Vikas Khatri

PUSTAK MAHAL®

Publishers
Pustak Mahal®

J-3/16 , Daryaganj, New Delhi-110002
☎ 23276539, 23272783, 23272784 • *Fax:* 011-23260518
E-mail: info@pustakmahal.com • *Website:* www.pustakmahal.com

Sales Centre

- 10-B, Netaji Subhash Marg, Daryaganj, New Delhi-110002
  ☎ 23268292, 23268293, 23279900 • *Fax:* 011-23280567
  E-mail: rapidexdelhi@indiatimes.com
- 6686, Khari Baoli, Delhi-110006
  ☎ 23944314, 23911979

Branches

Bengaluru: ☎ 080-22234025 • *Telefax:* 080-22240209
E-mail: pustak@airtelmail.in • pustak@sancharnet.in
Mumbai: ☎ 022-22010941, 022-22053387
E-mail: rapidex@bom5.vsnl.net.in
Patna: ☎ 0612-3294193 • *Telefax:* 0612-2302719
E-mail: rapidexptn@rediffmail.com
Hyderabad: *Telefax:* 040-24737290
E-mail: pustakmahalhyd@yahoo.co.in

ISBN 978-81-223-1263-8

Edition: 2011

Printed at : **Unique Colour Cartoon, Delhi**

Contents

❊❊

Introduction

The story of painting goes as far back as 20,000 years ago, to a time when Man had not yet learned to write. He looked around the world, and tried to reproduce what he saw in drawings. Man was just a caveman in those days, and the history of art began in caves.

Art has progressed through the ages. It has organized itself into different styles in terms of form, as well as content. Many painters belong to certain movements, giving different treatment to space, perspective, light and colour. History tells us of many great geniuses who led such movements, and revolutionized the world of art. A few examples are Edgar Degas, Vincent Van Gogh, and Pablo Picasso who created history by initiating great movements like Impressionism, Expressionism and Cubism.

This book presents to you some of these great painters whose works have stood the test of time. Inevitably, we had to make many reluctant omissions, and many names had to be left out for the lack of space. We have not included living painters either.

❋❋

Great Indian Painters

Amrita Shergill

One of the most promising Indian artists of the pre-colonial era; youngest ever and the only Asian to be elected as Associate of the Grand Salon in Paris.

Amrita Shergill was a renowned Indian painter. She was one of the most charismatic and promising Indian artists of the pre-colonial era. Most of her paintings reflect vividly her love for the country and more importantly her response to the life of its people.

Amrita Shergill was born in Hungary in 1913. Her father was a Sikh aristocrat and her mother was Hungarian. Both her parents were artistically inclined. Her father, Umrao Singh Majitha, was a Sanskrit Scholar and her mother, Marie Antoinette, was a pianist. Amrita spent her early childhood in the village of Dunaharasti in Hungary. In 1921 her family moved to Shimla. It was at this time that Amrita Shergil developed interest in painting. An Italian sculpture used to live in Shimla. In 1924, when the Italian sculpture moved to Italy, Amrita Shergill's mother too moved with her along with Amrita.

In Italy Amrita was enrolled at Santa Anunciata, a Roman Catholic institution. Amrita did not like the strict discipline of the Catholic school but on the flip side she was exposed to the works of the Italian masters and this further fanned her interest in painting. In 1927, Amrita Shergil returned to India and began taking lessons in painting under Ervin Backlay. But Ervin's insistence that Amrita should copy real life models exactly as she saw them irked Amrita and thus her painting stint under Ervin Backlay was short lived.

In 1929, at the age of sixteen, Amrita Shergil sailed to France to study Art. She took a degree in Fine Arts from the Ecole des Beaux Arts, Paris. She also learnt to speak and write French. It was in France that she started painting seriously. *The Torso*, one of her early paintings was a masterly study of a nude which stood out for its cleverness of drawing and bold modeling. In 1933, Amrita completed *Young Girls*. Critics and Art enthusiasts were so impressed by *Young Girls* that Amrita Shergill was elected as Associate of the Grand Salon in Paris. Amrita was the youngest ever and the only Asian to be honoured thus.

In 1934, Amrita Shergill returned to India and evolved her own distinct style which, according to her, was fundamentally Indian in subject, spirit, and technical expression. Now the subject of her paintings were the poor, the villagers and beggars. In 1937, Amrita Shergill went on a tour of South India. This gave her the opportunity to achieve the simplicity she always wanted in her paintings. In 1938, Amrita Shergill went to Hungary and married her cousin Victor Egan much to the opposition of her parents. She married purely for security reasons as she felt that she was essentially weak and needed someone to take care of her. In 1939, Amrita Shergill returned back to India and started painting again. After her return her health deteriorated and she died on December 6, 1941.

Famous Work: *Young Girls.*

❊❊

Jamini Roy

Developed a personal painting style inspired largely by traditional Indian folk and village arts, particularly those of Bengal. Through his paintings he gave expression to the scenes of everyday life of the people of rural Bengal.

Jamini Roy was one of the most significant and influential painters of the 20th century. He was born in a middle-class family in 1887 at Beliator village in Bankura district of Bengal. His father Ramataran Roy was an amateur artist who, after resignation from government service, spent the rest of his life in his village amidst the potters.

In 1903, at the age of sixteen, Jamini Roy came to Calcutta and studied at the Government School of Art. He learnt academic methods then in vogue in the West, and achieved his early fame as a portrait painter in the European tradition. However, soon Jamini Roy cultivated a personal painting style inspired largely by traditional Indian folk and village arts, particularly those of Bengal. Jamini Roy, through his oil paintings, gave expression to the scenes of every-day life of the people of rural Bengal.

For his paintings, Jamini Roy selected themes from joys and sorrows of everyday life of rural Bengal, religious theme like

Ramayana, Sri Chaitanya, Radha-Krishna and Jesus Christ, but he depicted them without narratives. Apart from this he painted scenes form the lives of the aboriginal Santhals, such as '*Santhals engaged in drum-beating*' '*Santhal Mother and Child*' '*Dancing Santhals*' etc.

In his career as an artist Jamini Roy earned fame by evolving his own language of painting which he termed as '*Flat Technique*'. Jamini Roy used cheap indigenous pigments for his art to make them within the reach of the affluent as well as the poor. Like the pata-painters of Bengal he proposed his own paintings from indigenous materials like lampblack, chalk-powder, leaves and creepers.

The exposition of Jamini Roy's works were first held in British India Street (Calcutta) in 1938. Jamini Roy's pictures became very popular during the 1940s and clientele included both the Bengali middle class and European community. In 1946, his work was exhibited in London and in 1953 in New York.

Jamini Roy was honoured with the Padma Bhushan in 1955. He died in 1972 in Calcutta.

Famous Work: *Santhal Boy with Drum.*

❋❋

Raja Ravi Varma

Raja Ravi Varma was one of the greatest painters in the history of Indian Arts. He brought Indian painting to the attention of the larger world; provided a vital link between the traditional Indian art and the contemporary art.

He is famous for his depiction of scenes from the epics of the Mahabharata and Ramayana. Raja Ravi Varma is most remembered for his paintings of beautiful sari clad women, who were portrayed as very shapely and graceful. He is considered as modern among traditionalists and a rationalist among moderns.

Raja Ravi Varma was born on April 29, 1848 in the royal palace of Kilimanoor, 25 miles from Thiruvananthapuram in Kerala, India. His parents were Umamba Thampuratti and Neelakandan Bhattathiripad. At the age of seven years he started drawing on the palace walls using charcoal. His uncle Raja Varma noticed the talent of Ravi Verma and gave him preliminary lessons in painting. At the age of 14, Ayilyam Thirunal Maharaja took him to Travancore Palace and he was taught water painting by the palace painter Rama Swamy Naidu. He was later given lessons in oil painting by a British painter, Theodor Jenson.

In 1873, Ravi Varma won the first prize at the Madras Painting Exhibition. He achieved worldwide acclaim after he won an award for an exhibition of his paintings at Vienna in 1873. He travelled throughout India in search of subjects. He often modelled Hindu

Goddesses on South Indian women, whom he considered beautiful. He stayed in the city of Bombay in Maharashtra for some years and drew many a beautiful Maharashtrian woman.

Ravi Varma is particularly noted for his paintings depicting episodes from the story of Dushyanta and Shakuntala, and Nala and Damayanti, from the Mahabharata. Raja Ravi Varma was fascinated by the power and forceful expression of European paintings, which came across to him as strikingly contrasting to stylized Indian artwork. His paintings are considered to be among the best examples of the fusion of Indian traditions with the techniques of European academic art.

Raja Ravi Varma died on October 2, 1906.

Famous Work: *Lady Lost in Thought.*

**

M F Husain

It wouldn't be wrong to say that painting was the life and soul of MF Husain. Blessed with one of the best gifts of God – art, Husain knew exactly how to make paintings speak for themselves. Over his tenure as a painter, he is claimed to have painted about 60, 000 paintings in topics as diverse as Mohandas K. Gandhi, Mother Teresa, the Ramayana, the Mahabharata, the British Raj, and motifs of Indian urban and rural life. Maqbool Fida Husain, popularly known as MF Husain, was, indeed, one of the prominent figures that India ever gave birth to. Known for his vigorous appreciation of God's creations, particularly humans, he went on to create some masterpieces, to be remembered for lifetime. Such was his scrutiny that he could portray circumstances and situations even with a pencil sketch. He is considered to be one such individual who blended ethnic and mythological themes to come up with luminous and incredible art forms.

Born in 1915, MF Husain came from a traditional Muslim background. He was born in Pandharpur, Bombay Presidency in British India. His mother, Zunaib died when he was one and a half years old. Thereafter, his father, Fida remarried a girl named Shireen and shifted to Indore. Husain was extremely close to his grandfather, from whom he drew his major inspiration.

Unfortunately, his grandfather could not accompany him for long as he passed away when Husain was just 6. Husain's formal education began at Sidhpur in Gujarat where he underwent 2 years of rigorous training in Indian religions. From here, he was transferred to an Islamic boarding school, Darul Talaba in Baroda. However, owing to his miserable performance, his father apprenticed him to a tailor and later to a draughtsman, hoping that he would pick up a profession. Interestingly, his father was very supportive towards his love for art. Seeing his possession and passion for art, he even gifted him an Agfa box camera. When Husain was just 16, his father rented a room in the neighbouring house where Husain could paint in complete privacy. He gained interest in English literature, courtesy his neighbour, Yavar, from where he started reading Shakespeare, John Ruskin, and books on British painters.

In 1935, Husain moved to Mumbai for the first time at the age of 20 and took admission in J.J. School of Arts. He earned his living by painting cinema hoardings and whenever he managed to save some money, he used to travel to Baroda, Surat, and Ahmedabad to paint landscapes. Since painting hoardings did not give him much of an earning, he tried his luck in other jobs. Amongst them, working at the toy factory proved to be the best paying job, where he was engaged in designing and building fretwork toys. After struggling and experiencing hardships for years in Mumbai, Husain finally received recognition in the late 1940s. Though in 1944, he received an offer from Fantasy for designing children's furniture and later in 1947 from Kamdars, a famous design company, his initial love remained painting.

In 1947, Husain's painting '*Sunhera Sansaar*' was exhibited at Bombay Art Society for the first time. The same year saw India's independence, after which, he decided to stay back in India. Soon after, Progressive Artists' Group (PAG) was formed by the artist Francis Newton Souza. Husain was amongst the early members and became the secretary of the group in 1949. This was just the first step towards the historic success that Husain went on to make later on. His first solo exhibition was held in Zurich in 1952, followed by a series of successful exhibitions across Europe and US. In 1971, he was sent a special invitation along with the legendary Pablo Picasso at the Sao Paulo Biennial. He was nominated at the Rajya Sabha for a term in 1986.

Besides earning the title of the most eminent and highest paid Indian painter, Husain also tried his hand at film direction. His first film '*Through the Eyes of a Painter*' produced in 1967 was victorious in bagging the Golden Bear at the Berlin Film Festival. Husain was so obsessed with the stunning Bollywood actress Madhuri Dixit that he considered her as his muse. He even went ahead to make a film with her, titled '*Gaja Gamini*' in 2000. Besides, Dixit remained the subject of his numerous paintings, which he titled '*Fida*'. Apart from Dixit, Husain also made a film titled '*Meenaxi: A Tale of Three Cities*' with Tabu, another Bollywood artiste, in 2004. Amrita Rao and Anushka Sharma are couple of other Bollywood actress who had cast a charm on Husain.

Husain was not just renowned for his exemplary paintings and portrayal of human figures, but he was also the center of controversies. His nude portraits of Hindu gods and goddesses or in an allegedly sexual manner captured a lot of eyeballs but all for the wrong reasons. Although the paintings were created in 1970, they did not become an issue till 1996, until they were published in a Hindi monthly magazine, *Vichar Mimansa*. The very instant response resulted in eight criminal complaints against Husain on the pretext of promoting enmity between Hindu goddesses, Durga and Saraswati, which was dismissed by Delhi High Court. Later in 1998, Hindu groups, like Bajrang Dal attacked his house and destroyed his paintings. The extent of the protests was such intense that his exhibition due in London was called off.

In 2004, after the release of his film '*Meenaxi: A Tale of Three Cities*' starring Tabu, he was objected by some Muslim organizations for using words directly from the Holy Quran in the Qawwali song 'Noor-un-Ala-Noor'. As a result, the movie was removed from cinema halls, just a day after its release. The complaint, lodged by the All-India Ulema Council, was supported by other Muslim organizations, such as the Milli Council, All-India Muslim Council, Raza Academy, Jamiat-ul-Ulema-e-Hind, and Jamat-e-Islami.

Yet again in February 2006, Husain again became the talk of the town when he again painted Bharatmata (Mother India) as a nude woman across the map of India with different Indian state names on various parts of the body. This nude portrayal was highly objected by Hindu Jagriti Samiti and Vishva Hindu Parishad, which resulted in the issue of a non-bailable warrant. Although Husain apologized and withdrew the painting from the auction, the painting was published on his official website. He left India in 2006 and went on a self-imposed exile, settling in Dubai. Later in 2010, he was offered the citizenship of Qatar, which he readily agreed. Thereafter, he had divided his time between homes in Qatar and London.

Husain had been honoured with India's three most prestigious civilian awards, Padma Shree in 1955, Padma Bhushan in 1973, and Padma Vibhushan in 1991, for his distinguished contribution in the field of art. His '*Battle of Ganga and Jamuna: Mahabharata 12*' successfully fetched *$ 1.6 million in 2008*, a world record at Christie's South Asian Modern and Contemporary Art sale. The same year, he was presented with the esteemed Raja Ravi Verma award by the Government of Kerala. He was also fortunate enough to have his name included in the list of '500 Most Influential Muslims in the World', released by the Royal Islamic Strategic Studies Center, Amman, Jordan.

Husain married Mehmoodabibi's daughter, Fazila on March 11th, 1941 in the presence of his father and some close friends. His wife was a constant support and inspiration who encouraged him to be firm in his beliefs.

Being unwell for over a month, Husain died of a heart attack in London. He breathed his last at the Royal Brompton Hospital on June 9, 2011; thus, bringing an end to the tenure of a genius and Picasso of India. His body was kept at Idara-e-Jaaferiya, a funeral parlor at Tooting, to let the public pay their homage to the legendary painter. He was buried on June 10, 2011 at the Brookwood Cemetery at Woking in Surrey, at the city's outskirts.

Famous Work: *Battle of Ganga and Jamuna: Mahabharata*

❋❋

Tyeb Mehta

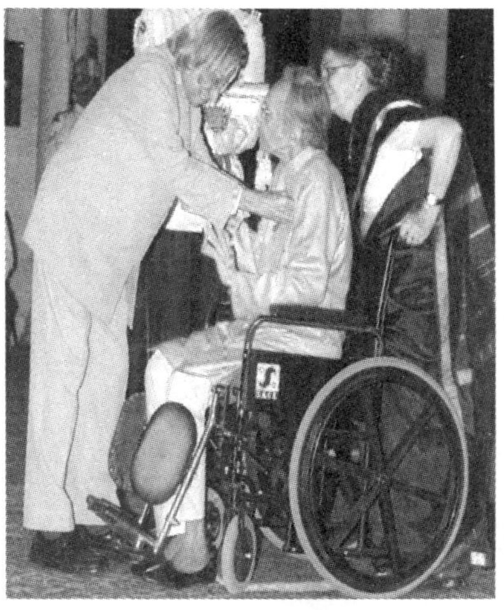

Held the record for the highest price for which an Indian painting has ever been auctioned; Recipient of Kalidas Samman and Padma Bhushan.

Tyeb Mehta was a well-known Indian artist, who was known all over the world for his brilliant painting. A multifaceted personality, he also dabbled in filmmaker and made a mark there. He held the record for the highest price for which an Indian painting has ever been sold, in a public auction. It was his triptych painting Celebration that, on being sold for 15 million Indian rupees ($300,000 USD), gave him this honour.

Tyeb Mehta was born on July 26, 1925 in Kapadvanj, Gujarat. He initially worked as a film editor in a cinema laboratory. However, his interest in painting took him to Sir J.J. School of Art, Bombay, where he studied painting from 1947 to 1952. There, Mehta also came in contact with Akbar Padamsee and became a close associate of the painters in the Progressive Artists' Group.

In 1954, Tyeb Mehta visited London and Paris for four months, following which he returned to India to concentrate on painting and sculpture. He took part in numerous group exhibitions and organized his first solo exhibition of drawings, paintings and sculptures at the Jehangir Art Gallery, Bombay, in 1959. He lived and worked in London from 1959 to 1965.

Tyeb Mehta returned to India in 1965 and lived in Delhi till 1968. In 1968, he visited United States, on a Rockefeller Fellowship. Around this time, he also dabbled in films. His film *'Koodal'* won the Film fare Critic's Award in 1970. In the 1980s, he worked as an Artist in Residence in Shantiniketan. He was also awarded the Kalidas Samman by the Madhya Pradesh Government in 1988.

In his lifetime, Tyeb Mehta participated in several international shows, like Ten Contemporary Indian Painters at Trenton in the US – 1965; Deuxieme Biennial Internationale de Menton – 1974; Festival Intemationale de la Peinture, Cagnes-Sur-Mer, France –1974; Modem Indian Paintings at Hirschhom Museum; Washington – 1982; and Seven Indian Painters at Gallerie Le Monde de U art, Paris – 1994.

On 2nd July 2009, Tyeb Mehta left for the holy abode, following a heart attack. He is survived by his wife – Sakina, a son and a daughter. Tyeb Mehta's large body of work, spanning over six decades, established him as one of the greatest names in the field of Modern Indian Art. His paintings raised numerous questions about the human condition, some of which remain unanswered till date.

Famous Work: *Celebration.*

❋❋

Manjit Bawa

Manjit Bawa, known for his striking portrayal of spirituality and simplicity through his paintings, was one of the highly-skilled artists India has had. Born in a small town of Dhuri, Punjab; it was tough-going for him to bring out his love for spirituality and nature onto the canvas, but thanks to his faith in the almighty and his elder brothers' faith in his abilities, who backed up his talent and supported him to pursue what he loved, Manjit not only realized his dreams but also made it big in the Indian world of painting. It was under Abani Sen that Manjit gained a distinct identity and sharpened his skills as a painter. Many of his works include depiction of spiritual figures and other figures in a non-cliched and subtle way that has set him apart from the rest. Drawing was his first love and he enjoyed doing it till the end.

Manjit Bawa was born in the year 1941 in a small town of Dhuri in Punjab. Being brought up on the mythological stories of Mahabharata, Ramayana, and the Puranas; poetry of a Punjabi poet Waris Shah, and readings from the Guru Granth Sahib; these became his source of inspiration. Also, being one with the nature from the early years was instrumental in making his zeal for painting all the more evident. Although his mother didn't approve of his interest on account of it not being a means to earn a livelihood, he made no qualms about it and believed that God would provide him with food and rest.

It was Manjit's elder brothers who backed him up and encouraged him to pursue his interest, and he ended up at School of Art, Delhi Polytechnic, New Delhi, and studied the finesse of arts from 1958 to 1963 under the guidance of his professors Somnath Hore, Rakesh Mehra, Dhanraj Bhagat, and B.C Sanyal. But it is to Abani Sen to whom Manjit gives credit – "But I gained an identity under Abani Sen. Sen would ask me to do 50 sketches every day, only to reject most of them. As a result I inculcated the habit of working continuously. He taught me to revere the figurative at a time when the entire scene was leaning in favour of the abstract. Without that initial training I could never have been able to distort forms and create the stylization you see in my work today."

Manjit never worked on demand but always followed his heart and mind, for he felt that everything has a time and place. He believed that by using the minimum essentials, he could extract the maximum effect out of his work. He was one of the few painters to break away from the use of grays and browns (a style made popular by the British) and opted for the exuberance of the natural colours like orange, blue, red, and green as he believed that bright colours are closer to the hearts of most Indians. He worked as a silk screen printer in Britain between 1964 and 1971, and also studied the art. After returning to India, when faced with the predicament of what to paint, as he couldn't settle for European style of painting; he decided to bring up his inspirations from the Indian mythology, poetry of Waris Shah, and readings from the holy book of Sikhs – Guru Granth Sahib; to canvas.

However, mythology and spiritual readings weren't the only source of his inspiration. Having visited most of the places and drawing their countryside onto the canvas; it was the simplicity of the colours and people from across the places, his interest for the flute that he learnt to play when he was young from the maestro Pannalal Ghosh himself, and being one with the nature at an early age that fascinated him to draw inspiration. It is precisely the reason why mythological figures, flute, and birds and animals kept appearing in many of his acclaimed paintings like *Krishna and the Bull*, *Ranjha*, *Govardhan*, *After 84*, *Heer,* etc. Also, he never hesitated to use figures of Kali and Shiva in his canvases as he deemed them as "the icons of my country". Emerging from early criticisms, over the time, his paintings have attracted Indian as well as international buyers.

Being in coma for almost 3 years, that resulted from a stroke in 2005; Manjit Bawa passed away on 29th December 2008 at his house in New Delhi. He is survived by his son, Ravi, and daughter, Bhawna.

Famous Work: *Krishna and the Bull.*

❋❋

Abanindranath Tagore

Born in the family of artists and painters, it was expected that Abanindranath Tagore would continue this legacy. And eventually he did, for the nation got its "Father of India's Modern Art" in the form of Abanindranath Tagore. Nephew of the world-renowned Bengali poet, musician, painter, and playwright Rabindranath Tagore, Abanindranath is celebrated for his attempts of modernizing the Mughal and Rajput styles of art to come up with an Indian touch replacing the Western models. Such was his devotion and affection towards painting that they travelled throughout the world and exhibited on various foreign lands. His modern Indian art saw several more painters being influenced, some of which include the notable and eminent Nandalal Bose, Asit Kumar Halder, Kshitindranath Majumder, Mukul Dey, Manishi Dey, and Jamini Roy.

Abanindranath Tagore was born into the distinguished Tagore family. He was born to Gunendranath Tagore, son of Girindranath Tagore, the second son of the famous "Prince" Dwarkanath Tagore, in Jorasanko in Calcutta in British India. His grandfather Girindranath and elder brother Gaganendranath were also prominent painters, who painted portraits and landscapes in

the European style. Additionally, Girindranath was a dramatist and musician apart from being just a painter. Born to such a talented and eminent family, Abanindranath himself grew up to excel in painting as well as writing. He attended the Sanskrit College from 1881 to 1889 where he gained interest for painting. As such, he took a few lessons from his classmate Anukul Chatterjee of Bhawanipur. Soon after he left college, he was married off to Suhasini Devi in 1889. Suhasini was the daughter of Bhujagendra Bhusan Chatterjee, a descendant of Prasanna Coomar Tagore. Soon after that, Abanindranath took admission in St. Xavier's College to study English, for one and a half years.

At about 25 years of age in 1897, Abanindranath started taking private painting lessons from an Italian artist, Signor Gilhardi, the Vice Principal of the Calcutta Government School of Art. He studied cast drawing, foliage drawing, pastel, and life study. Later, he attended the studio of Charles Palmer, an English painter from England, for three or four years to attain proficiency in oil painting and portraiture. It was during this period that he painted several eminent people in oils and achieved such perfection that he was able to complete a picture in just two hours. He even worked on the Krishna-Lal series, displaying a unique blend of European and Indian styles. The principal of Calcutta School of Art, E.B. Havell, was so impressed by his works that he offered him the post of Vice Principal at the same school. With this, began Abanindranath's journey of mastering several forms of arts and paintings. He studied Mughal and Rajput painting styles under the guidance of Havell.

Abanindranath followed his own traditions which were successfully depicted through his paintings. Though the British assumed his views to be spiritual, since they were a common part of British art at that time, several Britishers were sympathetic with his ideas. With this, his philosophies and ideologies started spreading in the West. Thus, began Abanindranath's contact with the outside world, beginning with various Asian artists, such as Chinese and Japanese calligraphic traditions. He learnt Japanese art under the guidance of the distinguished artist Okakura, who had come to India with Swami Vivekananda. Despite returning to Japan, Okakura sent Yokoyama Taikoan and Hilsida Shunso, two other famous Japanese artists, to India to help out Abanindranath in his training. Thus, he established a new national vocabulary in art and helped in regenerating the decadent art and aesthetic scene in India.

During his stint at the Government Art College, Abanindranath made stencil cutting and origami obligatory for students, replacing the once-proudly resting European paintings by Moghul and Rajput paintings on the school wall. Another interesting change that he brought about was the establishment of the department of fine arts. This gave his students an opportunity to meet reputed artists from all around the country and exchange their ideologies and principles. In the year 1907, Abanindranath established 'The Bengal School' and 'Indian School of Oriental Art' to promote his-style of painting at a national level. It was him who brought the modem art movement in Bengal and also proved that Indian artists had their own contribution to make to the world of painting. Later in 1913, Abanindranath was fortunate enough to exhibit his paintings in London and Paris. This further gave way for another painting exhibition in Japan in 1919. Abanindranath created over 500 paintings, some of which are displayed in Rabindra Bharati Society's collection at Jorasanko in Calcutta.

The world does not simply include Abanindranath's name in the list of versatile geniuses; this mastermind made a significant amount of contribution to literature as well in some important branches that declared him as a great litterateur in some time. He worked particularly on children's stories that spoke for themselves. Kshirer Putul, Buro Angla, Raj Kahini, and Sakuntala are some classics that still stimulate young children of Bengal. Other eminent works include Apankatha, Gharoa, Pathe Vipathe, Jorasankor Dhare, Bhutapatri, Nalaka, and Nahush. Abanindranath also penned essays on theories and philosophies of art that earned him great respect and admiration from artists and intellectuals.

Abanindranath Tagore passed away on December 5th in 1951 at the age of 80.

Famous Work: *Passing of Shah Jahan.*

❋❋

Nandalal Bose

Highly influenced by renowned artist Abanindranath Tagore, Nandalal Bose gave India its first experience of modern Indian style of painting. With an exemplary touch of renaissance in Indian painting, Nandalal Bose played a significant role in shaping up the modern face of traditional art through his deep thoughts of nationalism, philosophical inclination, awareness of the classical and folk art, all derived from his mentor and guide – Abanindranath Tagore. Apart from Tagore, E.B. Havell (principal of Calcutta Government Art School), Ananda Coomaraswami (famous art critic and historian), and Sister Nivedita (disciple of Swami Vivekananda) helped Bose in his transformation in his later years. Through his discoveries and experiences, he was able to present India with the modern face of art, while keeping the innate, indigenous roots intact.

Nandalal Bose was born to Purnachandra Bose and Kshetramani Devi in the obscure town of Haveli Kharagpur in Monghyr district of Bihar Province. His father was the manager of Kharagpur Tehsil of the Raja of Dharbhanga, while his mother was an orthodox woman with great beliefs in God and rituals. Nandalal was the third amongst five children. The eldest was brother Gokulchandra, followed by sister Kiran Bala. He was succeeded by sister Kamala and a younger brother Nimai. Nandalal was fortunate to inherit some of the painting virtues from his parents. While he attained the discipline and a hardworking nature from his father, his mother's interests for drawing and craftsmanship helped him move ahead. Thus, Nandalal gained interest in modeling images since childhood and created images of Durga, Ganesh, elephants, and bulls that were exhibited in fairs and festivals.

Such was Nandalal's fascination for coloured pictures that he searched for them in his old books and magazines during his

formal education. This drew more attention towards his hobby that was evident from his making sketches instead of taking down notes in school. At 15 years in 1897, Nandalal moved to Calcutta to pursue his higher studies. He took admission in Central Collegiate School and befriended Kantichandra Ghosh, who later became the famous translator of Omar Khayyam. He, later, joined General Assembly College to study for F.A. examination, though his first interest was still art. As expected, Nandalal failed to clear the examination and joined Metropolitan College. To his dismay, he failed to clear the examination this time as well. However, this did not reduce his love for art even a single bit.

After marriage, Nandalal was advised by his father-in-law, Prakashchandra Pal, to join Presidency College in 1905 to study commerce. However, he was still unable to concentrate on his studies due to his constant passion for drawing and painting. Not leaving his passion behind, Nandalal learnt model drawings, still life, and sauce painting from his cousin, Atul Mitra. He tried copying paintings of European painters, the most famous being Raphael's "*Madonna*". He was highly influenced by Raja Ravi Varma's paintings as well. One such example was Nandalal's original painting "*Mahasveta*", inspired by this great painter. While he was still in search of a mentor, he came across Abanindranath's paintings, "*Buddha*", "*Sujata*", and "*Bajra-Mukut*" that elated Nandalal instantly. He started regarding Tagore as his Guru and thus, worked on similar themes. Too shy to ask Abanindranath to accept him as a disciple, Nandalal took his classmate Satyen, along, whom he entrusted the task of speaking on his behalf. He had also taken with him the paintings that he had made. Not just Abanindranath, E.B. Havell who was present there too was taken aback by the paintings, especially his re-creation of the European painting "*Mahasveta*".

Abanindranath himself was an artist, apart from being just a teacher. Hence, he learned whatever came across from his students. This quality was perfectly absorbed by Nandalal. Though initially, Nandalal was guided by Harinarayan Basu and Iswari Prasad, Abanindranath himself started supervising him later on. At this time, Nandalal was his only student and served as his disciple for five years. He also earned a scholarship of Rs. 12. Abanindranath emphasized highly on the mythological stories of Ramayana and Mahabharatha. But Nandalal was extremely impressed by Buddha's and Bethala Panchavimshathi's stories. One such highly acclaimed work was "*Sati*". He accepted the modern western techniques of painting and portraiture, such as stained glass, gesso work, frescoes painting, and stencil cutting and printing. Nandalal, along with Surendranath Ganguly, was very close to his master Abanindranath, who proudly declared the two guys as his right and left hand. In 1907, the Indian Society of Oriental Art was formed by some English enthusiasts of Indian culture and few Indian artists and scholars. In an exhibition organized by the association, Nandalal displayed his two works "*Sati and Siva*" and "*Sati*". He was awarded a cash prize of Rs. 500 which he utilized for touring the entire nation, along with another artist, Priyanatha Sinha. Both of them visited Gaya, Banaras, Agra, Delhi, Mathura, and Brindavan. He was a common man's artist and wanted every person to have his painting in their homes. On his trip to Banupur, he sketched a number of pictures and sold each for 4 annas (25 paise). On discovering this act, Abanindranath went to Banupur and purchased the entire lot.

Apart from Abanindranath Tagore and E.B. Havell, Nandalal was highly inspired by Sister Nivedita as well, who was a dedicated disciple of Swami Vivekananda. Her initial training in painting was an insight for Indian culture that touched Nandalal to a great extent. She visited Calcutta with Jagdishchandra Bose to see Nandalal's paintings and was highly moved. She advised him to make paintings of Ajanta Frescoes. He went to Gwalior, assisted by Venkatappa Halder and Samarendra Gupta, and made copies of the frescoes. On her death, Nandalal stated "I have lost my guardian angel. I was introduced to Ramakrishna and Vivekananda by her".

Nandalal Bose drew inspiration from Rabindranath Tagore as well, who in turn was highly impressed by Nandalal's works. As such, Nandalal sketched many of Tagore's works, like

"*Chayanika*", "*Crescent Moon*", "*Gitanjali*", and "*Fruit Gathering*". He became the principal of Kala Bhavan (Art Department) at Shantiniketan in 1922. He used to prepare the stage for Tagore's plays. Both travelled to China, Japan, Malaya, and Burma in 1924. The two visited Ceylon ten years later in 1934.

Nandalal Bose was bestowed with several awards and accolades. He was conferred with the title "Deshikottama" by Vishvabharati University. He was honoured with the Silver Jubilee Medal by the Academy of Fine Arts in Calcutta. It was during those years that the Government of India started the awards of "Padma Shri", "Padma Bhushan", "Padma Vibhushan", and "Bharat Ratna". Jawaharlal Nehru asked Nandalal Bose to design the emblem of these awards. In the year 1954, he was honoured with the Padma Vibhushan award. He was the second artist to be elected as the Fellow of the Lalit Kala Akademi (India's National Academy of Art) in 1956. Later in 1965, the Asiatic Society of Bengal presented him with the Tagore Birth Cenetary Medal.

Nandalal Bose was married to 12-year old young girl, Sudhira Devi in 1903. The match was fixed by Nandalal's mother Kshetramani Devi during childhood who promised Sudhira Devi's mother to marry her as her future daughter-in-law. Though his mother passed away, the promise was fulfilled. His first daughter, Gauri, was born in 1907-08 who brought in good luck to Nandalal's life in terms of monetary aspects.

Nandalal Bose's health started deteriorating in his old age and he gave up all hopes of physical powers. Even his mental illness started playing hide and seek with him. Towards the end, he was unable to recollect faces ever. Bose breathed his last on April 16, 1966. Condolences poured in from people all over on the demise of a master artist.

Famous Work: *Sati.*

❋❋

Bikash Bhattacharjee

Bikash Bhattacharjee, holder of two of the most prestigious awards: National Award and Padma Shri amongst many others, is a renowned Indian painter known for his spectacular depiction of reality as well as surrealism. Despite being born in Kolkata struck amidst a political turmoil and losing his father at an early age didn't stop him from discovering his true calling. Supported by his mother, a lifelong friend in Katayun Saklat (his classmate), and Arun Basu (his college teacher), who sharpened his existing talent, Bikash brought out the very best in him. His remarkable quality of portraying real life objects onto the canvas with an immaculate exactness had the experts and audience stunned to their senses alike. Over the years, he even took up a role as a teacher and continued the same for more than a decade. His paintings reflected the life of average middle-class Bengali – their aspirations, superstitions, hypocrisy and corruption, and even the violence that is rife to Kolkata.

Bikash Bhattacharjee was born on 21st June, 1940 in North Calcutta, in a politically turbulent West Bengal. Having lost his father at the age of 6, it wasn't exactly easy growing up with crumbling riches of his household and Hindu-Muslim riots that led to the partition of Bengal and eventually, to national independence. Having seen pretty much everything which children of this age aren't ideally supposed to be seeing, agonizing sights of huge masses flooded over railway stations and even deaths during the post independence traumatic era, Bikash had developed a deep sense of insecurity and empathy for the underprivileged. One day as usual, strolling down the dark neighbourhood lanes in search of something unknown, he came across a sit-and-draw competition and apparently became the first runner up in it. Encouraged by his mother, it quickly dawned on him where his future lied and in pursuit of it Bikash joined Indian College of Art and Draftsmanship in 1958 and completed it in 1963, with a diploma in fine arts. A year later, he became a member of the Society of Contemporary Artists.

Despite a teaching career of more than a decade: 4 years at Indian College of Art and Draftsmanship and 9 years at Government College of Art & Craft; it was Bikash's surreal painting career that made him a name he is today. Coming face to face with harsh realities at an early childhood; he possessed an exceptional grasp over depicting objects and people the way they appeared in real life: a quality that remained his strong suit till the end. Bikash always thought of himself as an incurable optimist and the same could not keep itself from being manifested in the way he drew. In addition to this, inclusion of feminine beauty with a balance of spiritualism and sensuality in quite a lot of his work was evidence to his preoccupation to the same.

Bikash had tasted success early on during his painting career with the *Doll series*, followed by the *Durga series*. It was in the year 1965 that his solo exhibition was held at Kolkata. Along with the paintings depicting hyper-realism, he was also exceptional in portrait paintings and it's visible in his paintings of other artists like Rabindranath Tagore, Satyajit Ray, Samaresh Babu, and Indira Gandhi. He also created painted illustrations for a novel on the life of Ramkinker Baij. Indian recognition wasn't all he got; as his works even gained an international audience when they were exhibited across the countries and cities like Paris, London, New York, Yugoslavia, Czechoslovakia, Romania, and Hungary. It was his unrestrictive quality to work with an array of mediums like oil on canvas and board, tempera paint, pastels, water colours, crayons, and pencils and blending in realism with surrealism that gave him mastery over the art.

It was in 2000 that Bikash suffered a cerebral attack that left him paralyzed, unable to paint. On 18th December 2006, he passed away following a prolonged illness. He is survived by his wife Parbati, a son and a daughter.

Famous work: *Fantasy Show, Doll Series.*

❋❋

Binod Behari Mukherjee

"The person who is not roused by a pulsating image, a small touch or sound, can make no sense of the word 'beauty'. A person who neither knows, nor thinks beyond his worldly needs has no use for beauty."

For someone who spent a majority of his life with weak sight and finally became blind at the age of 50 to produce such an enviable body of works in the field of art and literature, not getting deterred by disability, is the very personification of the above mentioned quote. A quote which he once wrote aptly describes him as someone who understands beauty and life, for the works of Binod Behari Mukherjee are themselves representation of beauty and life in all its forms. His work had always overflowed the banks of tradition and were based on his experience and understanding of nature. His murals, which display his understanding and the essence of environmental and architectural nuances, make him one of the stalwarts of Indian visual arts movement.

Binod Behari Mukherjee was born into a highly literate family in the year 1904. During his childhood, he suffered from an illness that affected his vision, making him blind in one eye and myopic in the other. As such, he was not able to pursue systematic education and instead, had to complete his schooling from a Brahmacharya Ashram. But he developed a passion for painting and in order to hone his talent, he, in 1919, joined Santiniketan's Kala Bhavan for a Diploma in Fine Arts, where Nandalal Bose and Rabindranath Tagore were his gurus, with the former being his art teacher. Mukherjee excelled in painting, a talent that was recognized and encouraged by his teachers. In 1925, he became an art teacher himself at the same institution and taught till 1949, inspiring many students, who would later become celebrated artists like Jahar Dasgupta, K.G. Subramanyan, sculptor & printmaker Somnath Hore, designer Riten Majumdar and filmmaker Satyajit Ray. During this period, along with teaching, Mukherjee also began painting and sculpting extensively, proving this to be one of his most creative periods.

Mukherjee also began to travel widely to understand and experience the various forms of nature. In 1949, he was invited to the position of a curator of the Nepal government museum which he accepted. During his stay in Nepal, Mukherjee did a series of drawings and watercolours that captured the rich art of the kingdom. After his return from Nepal in 1951, he taught at the Banasthali Vidyapith, a women's educational center in Rajasthan for a year after finally, settling in Missouri in 1952, along with his wife Leela. Together, they started an art training school over there to provide training to artists and art teachers. The verdant mountains of the Himalayas inspired him to make landscape his major subject once again, creating works that captured the transient aspect of nature with mountains and mists being the dominant motifs. In 1958, Mukherjee joined Shantiniketan's Kala Bhavan again as a faculty and later became its principal. All these years, his eyesight was gradually failing and following an eye operation in 1956, Mukherjee completely lost his sight at the age of 52. But as with all great artists, physical disabilities couldn't stop him from his creative pursuits, even if it was the eyesight, perhaps the most important tool of an artist. But here he proved that it is the inner vision that makes a great artist and he began to paint, draw and sculpt depending only upon this quality to see from the "inner eye".

At Shantiniketan, Mukherjee developed a style that veered away from overt symbolism of literary subjects and mythological descriptions to portraying simple representations of his surroundings, capturing the landscape and life in and around the university. He gave more importance to colour, line and texture. His sketches, watercolours and drawings were a celebration of life. Apart from nature, Mukherjee took his inspiration from Chinese and Japanese art as well. During this time, he also began experimenting with mural paintings, which he felt were more expressive as murals were intricate and descriptive, allowing him to present his view of life more comprehensively. In 1940, Mukherjee painted a mural in the ceiling of the hostel dormitory, which is considered to be the first of his significant murals. This mural represented the landscape and essence of local villages that had been presented, as a critic puts it, in a "continuous web of intricate images and unfolds it around the central pond to the four corners of the ceiling, constantly shifting the perspective and focus of the viewer".

With time, Mukherjee adopted different media to work on from sketches, calligraphy and watercolours at the start to tempera on wood and then gradually moving on to silk, textile block prints and finally, moving onto paper cuts. After losing his eyesight, he also started to write, taking the activity more seriously than before, writing about his experiences, history of art education and a series of incisive studies. The latter was published posthumously as a book. But the book that brought him fame as a writer in Bengali was '*Chitrakor*' published in 1979, a collection of autobiographical pieces. '*Chitrakor*' was landmark work of literature that won two awards in 1980, namely the Rabindra Puraskar and the Bhartiya Bhasha Parishad Award. Satyajit Ray who considered Binod Behari Mukherjee his mentor and inspiration was so impressed by the latter's paper cut works called '*The Inner Eye*', that he made a small documentary on this work with the same title in the year 1973. This documentary was instrumental in bringing the works of Binod Behari to a wider audience.

Vishva Bharti University recognizing his contribution in the fields of arts and literature, in the year 1977, awarded Mukherjee the honourary doctorate degree. He was also honoured with Padma Vibhushan in 1974, India's second highest civilian award. In the year 1980, he was also bestowed with the Rabindra Puraskar and the Bhartiya Bhasha Parishad Award for his work '*Chitrakor*'.

The legendary painter of Indian modern art, Binod Behari Mukherjee left for the heavenly abode in 1980, at the age of 76. Despite being visually impaired, Mukherjee was never withheld by his inability to see and went on to create some of the most exquisite works that we cherish till date.

Famous Work: *Chitrakor.*

❋❋

B C Sanyal

Bhabesh Chandra Sanyal, better known to us as B C Sanyal, is considered to have ushered in the era of modernism in Indian art. A painter, a sculptor and a teacher of art to three generations of artists, B. C. Sanyal lived through the different partitions that India went through in 1905, 1947 and 1971. This was also the time when art in India experienced several developments, Bhabesh Chandra Sanyal playing an important role in bringing about these developments. B. C. Sanyal was raised by his mother and he often referred to her as his mother as the chief inspiration in his life and career as an artist. He shifted base to Delhi from Assam after India's independence and remained in the Indian capital for the rest of his life.

Bhabesh Chandra Sanyal was born on April 22, 1901 in the town of Dhubri in Assam. Though he was only a little child, he did experience and also understood the sentiments attached with the Partition of Bengal in the year 1905. Soon after, tragedy struck the Sanyal family when his father died when B. C. Sanyal was only six years of age. His mother had to raise young Sanyal single handedly, which she did efficiently. In her leisure time, she used to give in to her hobby of making dolls which was from where the sculptor in him was born. Sanyal enrolled at the Government College of Art & Craft in Calcutta, where he took training under J P Ganguly and Percy Brown. At the age of 19 in the year 1920,

Sanyal became a student of the Serampore College of Art and it was in this institution that he spent the next six years of his life, first learning painting and then becoming a teacher of painting and sculpture. It was B C Sanyal's personal distinct style of art which caught the attention of his peers and teachers.

B C Sanyal was a teacher of art and sculpture at the Serampore College of Art from 1920 to 1926. His career got a fresh start in the year 1929 when a Punjabi firm named Krishna Plaster Works appointed Sanyal in their team travelling to Lahore. He was given the task to mould a bust of India's hero in the freedom struggle Lala Lajpat Rai prior to the beginning of the Lahore session of the Indian National Congress. After his work with Krishna Plaster Works came to an end, Sanyal stayed back in Lahore and took up employment at the Mayo School of Arts in Lahore. After teaching art for a few years, he went on to become the vice principal of the Mayo School, a position that he held till 1936. Though he did not want to do it, Sanyal was forced to resign from the vice principal's post at Mayo School of Arts and leave the institution in the year 1936 when differences arose between him and British authorities who controlled the Mayo School. Some of Sanyal's prominent students from Mayo School of Arts were Krishnen Khanna and Satish Gujral who went on to become prominent figures of the art world during the modernism of post independence art and sculpture. Though he left the institution, Sanyal did not leave Lahore immediately. Rather, he set up a studio which also functioned as a school within the premises of the Forman Christian College and named it the Lahore College of Art. A few years later, the premises of the Lahore College of Art was shifted to the famous Dayal Singh Mansions of the city, after Sanyal received positive response and a huge turnout of the most popular artistes when he organized an exhibition in the basement of the building. Sanyal remained as the teacher at the Lahore College of Art till India's independence in 1947, after which he permanently migrated to Delhi.

After 1947, Sanyal left Lahore and settled with his wife Snelata in Delhi. His place of work, the 26 Gole Market area of Delhi soon became famous as the hub for established artists and students of art in the city. Sanyal set up the Delhi Shilpi Chakra in Gole Market in association with other friends from the world of art. The group was influential in bringing about a much needed change in the type of contemporary art produced from not only

Delhi but also from several places across North India. From the year 1949, Sanyal participated in a number of programs across the world, from the Salon de Mai in Paris in 1949, to the Venice Biennale in 1953. He returned to India to join as the professor of art in Delhi Polytechnic the same year. After the completion of his term in Delhi Polytechnic, Sanyal joined the All India Fine Arts and Crafts Society (AIFACS) and became the secretary of the Lalit Kala Akademi (LKA) from 1960 to 1969. After 1969, Sanyal was appointed the vice chairman of the Lalit Kala Akademi.

Sanyal loved watercolours and oil paintings and the better part of his works are in either of the two. '*The Veiled Figure*', drawn in memory of his mother was a path-breaking success. Other important works by Sanyal were '*Way to Peace*', '*The Flying Scarecrow*', '*Despair*' and '*Cow Herd*'. He portrayed the lives of the underprivileged and the downtrodden of the society in his works of art. The simple human life and the struggles that mankind had to engage in for living were his most preferred themes in painting. The works of Sanyal is presently housed at the National Gallery of Modern Art in New Delhi. Apart from painting and sculpture, Sanyal also acted in a film titled '*Dance of the Wind*' in 1997. During the later stages of life, Sanyal travelled to Himachal Pradesh and settled there for a while in an attempt to set up the Andretta artists' resort and the Nora Center for the Arts in the resort. He was so involved in the project along with friend Norah Richards that he started exhibitions and sale of his own paintings to raise money for the purpose.

Bhabesh Chandra Sanyal's genius was recognized by the Indian government which awarded him duly. The painter, sculptor and art teacher received a number of awards towards the later part of his career:

- Lalit Kala Akademi Fellowship for lifetime achievement by the National Academy of Fine Arts in India in the year 1980.
- The Padma Bhushan in 1984.
- An honourary citizenship of Baltimore from the US government in the year 1989.
- Gagan Abani Puraskar by Visva Bharati University in 1993.

- Sankar Dev Award by government of Assam in 1999.
- Special postage stamp issued by Indian government to observe the centenary year of B C Sanyal's birth in 2000.
- IGNCA, New Delhi released a DVD on B C Sanyal along with Elizabeth Brunner in Great Masters on April 22, 2001.
- Special exhibition with more than 170 artists participating was organized on April 22, 2001 by IGNCA as part of the centenary birthday celebrations of B C Sanyal.

Bhabesh Chandra Sanyal died on August 9, 2003 in New Delhi aged 103. He remained active till the last years of his life practicing lithography even at the age of 101. It was a minor short term illness that took away B. C. Sanyal's life in the year 2003. The artist was survived by his wife Snelata and their daughter Amba Sanyal.

Famous Work: *Way to Peace.*

❋❋

Mukul Chandra Dey

An established artist and one of the brightest students from Santiniketan during Rabindranath Tagore's era, Mukul Chandra Dey was the first Indian to go overseas to study printmaking as a form of art and profession. Mukul Chandra Dey travelled to different cities across America and Japan to learn printmaking from established artists in the western world. Often Rabindranath Tagore accompanied his student during these journeys, both of them putting up as guests of imminent people from the world of art. Mukul Chandra Dey's journey abroad was not only for exploration of the western art world, but also to learn various nuances of art from the experts. Mukul Chandra Dey returned to India where he had spent much of his childhood and took up drypoint-etching as a profession. He is considered to have established this art form in India.

Mukul Chandra Dey was born on July 23, in the year 1895, in the Sridharkhola region of Bangladesh. Nothing much about his childhood has been recorded and therefore nothing about Mukul Chandra Dey's life in Bangladesh is known. It is from his learning years in Santiniketan that most of us have become aware of the extraordinary talent of Mukul Chandra Dey. He took lessons in Santiniketan from none other than the maestro Rabindranath Tagore himself and it is said that Dey was one of the most popular students in Santiniketan and also a favourite with Tagore. Many of his later travels to study art around the world were made in the company of Tagore who became Mukul Chandra Dey's mentor.

After completing his studies in Santiniketan, Mukul Chandra Dey made his first travel overseas to America in the year 1916. The purpose for which he had left for America was to study printmaking and later adapt the same as his profession. He was the first Indian to study printmaking abroad. After spending a few months in America, Mukul Chandra Dey travelled to Japan in the same year, this time to learn and master the technique of the art of etching. In America, he settled in Chicago to train under the expert hands of Bertha E Jaques and James Blanding Sloane. American artist Roi Partridge and his family were also constant companions of Mukul Chandra Dey during his stay in the country. It was within days of his stay in Chicago that Mukul Chandra Dey became a member of the Chicago Society of Etchers, a membership that he retained throughout his life even after he left America, travelled to Japan and subsequently returned to India to start his own work.

His mentor Rabindranath Tagore accompanied Mukul Chandra Dey in his journeys to Japan. The master and the student settled in the Japanese cities of Tokyo and Yokohama for their research on etching and printmaking. Mukul Chandra Dey got his initial lessons in Japan from stalwarts in the world of art Yokoyama Taikan and Kanzan Shimomura. Both Rabindranath Tagore and Mukul Chandra Dey stayed in Yokohama as the guests of the famous silk merchant Tomitaro Hara. His sprawling complex the Sankeien housed the best collection of Nihonga Japanese and Chinese paintings. The works of the renowned Sesshu Toyo were also housed at Sankein, thus providing Mukul Chandra Dey an opportunity to take a look at some of the most wonderful pieces of creations in art.

Mukul Chandra Dey spent only one year in America and Japan, returning to India in the year 1917 to put to work the different art forms which he had learnt in both countries. Etching was the personal favourite of Mukul Chandra Dey and he made etchings as a form of fine art. In order to make a living out of painting, Mukul Chandra Dey started drawing portraits of the famous and the rich in India. Sometimes he turned these portraits into etchings, a practice which helped Mukul Chandra Dey to practice his choice of art as well as to earn a living out of the passion of his life. He stayed in India for three years before making a journey to Europe.

In the year 1920, Mukul Chandra Dey set out on a journey abroad yet again. This time too it was for the purpose of studying different forms of painting. His first stop in Europe was London where Mukul Chandra Dey enrolled at the Slade School of Fine Art, learning under Professor Henry Tonks and then at the Royal College of Art in London. Throughout his stay in London, Mukul Chandra Dey practiced etching and engraving under established English artists Muirhead Bone and Frank Short. Though he had always dreamt of visiting Paris at some point of time in his life to complete his education in etching and printmaking, he never did so, choosing to return to Santiniketan following the words of his much loved teacher and world famous sculptor Stanislaw Szukalski. A report claims that it was the Polish sculptor who had convinced Mukul Chandra Dey to relinquish his Paris dreams. Stanislaw Szukalski was much impressed with the drawings of Mukul Chandra Dey and told him that just going to Paris or for that matter any other European nation will not help anything in his style. Rather, Mukul Chandra Dey may get engulfed in the culture of Paris, a city which has the capacity of brainwashing the people of all regions around the world with its glamour and grandeur!

Mukul Chandra Dey's mentor Rabindranath Tagore was also against the idea of his pupil travelling and settling in any European city. Needless to say, Tagore was very happy when the former returned to India forever. Mukul Chandra Dey went on to introduce the concept of drypoint etching in the world of Indian art, a concept popular only in European art. What made the works of Mukul Chandra Dey so different from his contemporaries was the fact that he used the concept of drypoint etching to portray objects that were very familiar to Indian pattern of life. For instance, the subjects of his paintings always revolved around the rivers and streams, the baul singers, the marketplace of Calcutta and the distinct ways of life of the Santhal tribes which lived in and around the district of Birbhum in West Bengal.

The drypoint etchings may have used a concept seen only in the West, but the subjects were always as seen near Santiniketan, his alma mater. Therefore, Mukul Chandra Dey's art pieces gradually became popular not only with critics but also among the common man. Moreover, Rabindranath Tagore also provided Mukul Chandra Dey the opportunity to experiment with other different art forms when he opened the Vichitra Club in Jorasanko, a club that was set up to encourage young and upcoming artists to give expressions to their ideas.

Keeping in mind his growing popularity, Mukul Chandra Dey was offered the position of the Principal of the Government School of Art in Calcutta in the year 1928. He was the first Indian to hold this position of importance in the art circuit of Calcutta. His contribution to the school, apart from improving the quality of art produced, lay in the fact that he made it possible for girls to become a part of the institution of art. Prior to Mukul Chandra Dey's stint as principal, the Government School of Art was open to only boys.

Mukul Chandra Dey was best known for drypoint etchings of villagers from Bengal. Sometimes, Mukul Chandra Dey painted drypoint etching creations with watercolours, coloured pencils or mere ink. Dey continued to paint the portraits of famous people from India and abroad, a trait which he had started during the early stages of his career. Some of the most famous personalities that Mukul Chandra Dey painted are Mohandas Karamchand Gandhi, Rabindranath Tagore, Albert Einstein, members of the Tata family and Josephine MacLeod.

Mukul Chandra Dey died on March 1, 1989. The artist's home in Santiniketan, Chitralekha, has been transformed into the Mukul Dey Archives by the Government of Bengal.

Mukul Chandra Dey's paintings and other works of art are housed at museums across different cities in India and abroad. The Indian Mueum in Kolkata, the National Gallery of Modern Art in Mumbai, the National Gallery of Art in New Delhi and the Victoria and Albert Museum in London are some places where we will find the maximum collection of Mukul Chandra Dey art pieces.

Famous Works: *Portraits of Mohandas Karamchand Gandhi and Rabindranath Tagore.*

❋❋

Great International Painters

Fra Angelico

Fra Angelico, (1935-1455), Italian painter of the early Renaissance, who combined the life of a devout friar with that of an accomplished painter. He was called Angelico (Italian for "angelic") and Beato (Italian for "blessed") because the paintings he did were of calm, religious subjects and because of his extraordinary personal piety.

Originally named Guido di Pietro, Angelico was born in Vicchio, Tuscany. He entered a Dominican convent in Fiesole in 1418 and about 1425 became a friar using the name Giovanni da Fiesole. Although his teacher is unknown, he apparently began his career as an illuminator of missals and other religious books. He began to paint altarpieces and other panels; among his important early works are the *Madonna of the Star* (1428-1433, San Marco, Florence) and *Christ in Glory Surrounded by Saints and Angels* (National Gallery, London), which depicts more than 250 distinct figures. Among other works of that period are two of the *Coronation of the Virgin* (San Marco and Louvre, Paris) and a *Deposition and Last Judgment* (San Marco). His mature style is first seen in the *Madonna of the Linen Weavers* (1433, San Marco), which features a border with 12 music-making angels.

In 1436 the Dominicans of Fiesole moved to the convent of San Marco in Florence, which had recently been rebuilt by Michelozzo. Angelico, sometimes aided by assistants, painted many frescoes for the cloister, chapter house, and entrances to the 20 cells on the upper corridors. The most impressive of these are the *Crucifixion, Christ as a Pilgrim,* and *Transfiguration.* His altarpiece for San Marco (1439) is one of the first representations of what is known as a *Sacred Conversation:* the Madonna flanked by angels and saints who seem to share a common space.

In 1445 Angelico was summoned to Rome by Pope Eugenius IV to paint frescoes for the now destroyed Chapel of the Sacrament in the Vatican. In 1447, with his pupil Benozzo Gozzoli, he painted frescoes for the cathedral in Orvieto. His last important works, frescoes for the chapel of Pope Nicholas in the Vatican, are *Scenes from the Lives of Saints Stephen and Lawrence* (1447-1449), probably painted from his designs by assistants. From 1449 to 1452 Angelico was prior of his convent in Fiesole. He died in the Dominican convent in Rome on March 18, 1455.

Angelico combined the influence of the elegantly decorative Gothic style of Gentile da Fabriano with the more realistic style of such Renaissance masters as the painter Masaccio and the sculptors Donatello and Ghiberti, all of whom worked in Florence. Angelico was also aware of the theories of perspective proposed by Leon Battista Alberti. Angelico's representation of devout facial expressions and his use of colour to heighten emotion are particularly effective. His skill in creating monumental figures, representing motion, and suggesting deep space through the use of linear perspective, especially in the Roman frescoes, mark him as one of the foremost painters of the Renaissance.

Famous Work: *Deposition of Christ.*

❋❋

Sandro Botticelli

Sandro Botticelli, real name Alessandro di Mariano Filipepi (1445-1510), one of the leading painters of the lorentine Renaissance. He developed a highly personal style characterized by elegant execution, a sense of melancholy, and a strong emphasis on line; details appear as sumptuous still lifes.

Botticelli was born in Florence, the son of a tanner. His nickname was derived from Botticello ("little barrel"), either the nickname of his elder brother or the name of the goldsmith to whom Sandro was first apprenticed. Later he served an apprenticeship with the painter Fra Filippo Lippi. He worked with the painter and engraver Antonio del Pollaiuolo, from whom he gained his sense of line; he was also influenced by Andrea del Verrocchio.

Botticelli had his own workshop by 1470. He spent almost all of his life working for the great families of Florence, especially the Medici family, for whom he painted portraits, most notably the *Giuliano de' Medici* (1475-1476, National Gallery of Art, Washington, D.C.). *Adoration of the Magi* (1476-1477, Uffizi, Florence) was painted on commission (though not for the Medicis), and contains likenesses of the Medici family. As part of the brilliant intellectual and artistic circle at the court of Lorenzo de' Medici, Botticelli was influenced by its Christian Neoplatonism, which tried to reconcile classical and Christian views. This synthesis may be the theme of two larger panels commissioned for Medici villas and now in the Uffizi, *Primavera* (1478) and *Birth of Venus* (after 1482). While scholars have not yet conclusively deciphered these paintings, their slender elegant figures, which form abstract linear patterns bathed in soft golden light, may depict Venus as a symbol of both pagan and Christian love.

Botticelli also painted religious subjects, especially panels of the Madonna, such as the *Madonna of the Magnificat* (1480s), *Madonna of the Pomegranate* (1480s), and *Coronation of the Virgin* (1490), all in the Uffizi, and *Madonna and Child with Two Saints* (1485, Staatliche Museen, Berlin). Other religious works include *Saint Sebastian* (1473-1474, Staatliche Museen) and a fresco, *Saint Augustine* (1480, Church of the Ognissanti, Florence). In 1481 Botticelli was one of several artists chosen to go to Rome to decorate the walls of the Sistine Chapel in the Vatican. There he executed *The Youth of Moses,* the *Punishment of the Sons of Corah,* and the *Temptation of Christ.*

In the 1490s, when the Medici were expelled from Florence and the fanatic Dominican monk Girolamo Savonarola preached austerity and reform, Botticelli experienced a religious crisis. His subsequent works, such as the *Pietà* (early 1490s, Museo Poldi Pezzoli, Milan) and especially the *Mystic Nativity* (1490s, National Gallery, London) and *Mystic Crucifixion* (1496, Fogg Art Museum, Cambridge, Massachusetts), reflect an intense religious devotion.

Famous Work: *Birth of Venus.*

❊❊

Hieronymus Bosch

Bosch, Hieronymus (1450-1516), one of the most famous of the Netherlandish artists, known for his enigmatic panels illustrating complex religious subjects with fantastic, often demonic imagery.

The documents about Bosch indicate that he followed the predictable life of a prominent Roman Catholic artist in Hertogenbosch, a provincial but prosperous town located in the modern Netherlands close to the Belgian border. His father and grandfather were both painters in the same town before him, and apparently Bosch lived all his life there. He married a local woman and joined the lay organization of the Confraternity of Notre Dame. Bosch was responsible for designing a stained-glass window, among several other works, for the town church. His art was well-known outside Hertogenbosch during his lifetime.

References to astrology, folklore, witchcraft, and alchemy, in addition to the theme of the Antichrist and episodes from the lives of exemplary saints, are all woven together by Bosch into a labyrinth of late medieval Christian iconography. Scholars differ in their interpretation of Bosch's art, but most agree that his pictures show a preoccupation with the human propensity for sin in defiance of God, as well as with God's eternal damnation of lost souls in hell as a fateful consequence of human folly.

Stylistically, Bosch worked in a manner called *alla prima,* a method of applying paint freely on a preliminary ground of brownish paint. He was familiar with Dutch manuscript paintings and with foreign prints, and many of his images can be traced to these sources.

Dated works by Bosch do not exist and, of those panels that bear his signature, many might have been by followers. His pictures were widely imitated well into the later 16th century. During the 1550s, a veritable Boschian revival occurred in Antwerp that involved artists such as Pieter Huys and even Pieter Bruegel the Elder, who openly made variations of his paintings. Descriptions of some of his works were written by 16th-century Spanish nobleman Don Felipe Guevara. Among other sources, these have aided modern art historians in determining Bosch's authentic works.

Among the dozens of Boschian paintings, the autograph works generally accepted as his include the following: *The Marriage at Cana* (Museum Boymans-van Beuningen, Rotterdam), *The Seven Deadly Sins* (Prado, Madrid), *Crucifixion* (Musées Royaux des Beaux-Arts, Brussels), *The Hay Wain* (Prado), *The Death of the Miser* (National Gallery of Art, Washington, D.C.), *The Temptation of Saint Anthony* (Museu Nacional de Arte Antiga, Lisbon), *The Garden of Earthly Delights* (Prado), *The Adoration of the Magi* (Prado), and *Christ Carrying the Cross* (Museum voor Schone Kunsten, Ghent).

Famous Work: *Garden of Earthly Delights.*

❊❊

Leonardo da Vinci

Leonardo da Vinci (1452-1519), Florentine artist, one of the great masters of the High Renaissance, celebrated as a painter, sculptor, architect, engineer, and scientist. His profound love of knowledge and research was the keynote of both his artistic and scientific endeavours. His innovations in the field of painting influenced the course of Italian art for more than a century after his death, and his scientific studies—particularly in the fields of anatomy, optics, and hydraulics—anticipated many of the developments of modern science.

Leonardo was born in the small town of Vinci, in Tuscany (Toscana), near Florence. He was the son of a wealthy Florentine notary and a peasant woman. In the mid-1460s the family settled in Florence, where Leonardo was given the best education that Florence, a major intellectual and artistic center of Italy, could offer. He rapidly advanced socially and intellectually. He was handsome, persuasive in conversation, and a fine musician and improviser. About 1466 he was apprenticed as a *garzone* (studio boy) to Andrea del Verrocchio, the leading Florentine painter and sculptor of his day. In Verrocchio's workshop Leonardo was introduced to many activities, from the painting of altarpieces and panel pictures to the creation of large sculptural projects in marble and bronze. In 1472 he was entered in the painter's guild of Florence, and in 1476 he was still considered Verrocchio's assistant. In Verrocchio's

Baptism of Christ (1470, Uffizi, Florence), the kneeling angel at the left of the painting is by Leonardo.

In 1478 Leonardo became an independent master. His first commission, to paint an altarpiece for the chapel of the Palazzo Vecchio, the Florentine town hall, was never executed. His first large painting, *The Adoration of the Magi* (begun 1481, Uffizi), left unfinished, was ordered in 1481 for the Monastery of San Donato a Scopeto, Florence. Other works ascribed to his youth are the so-called *Benois Madonna* (1478, Hermitage, Saint Petersburg), the portrait *Ginevra de' Benci* (1474, National Gallery, Washington, D.C.), and the unfinished *Saint Jerome* (1481, Pinacoteca, Vatican).

About 1482 Leonardo entered the service of the duke of Milan, Ludovico Sforza, having written the duke an astonishing letter in which he stated that he could build portable bridges; that he knew the techniques of constructing bombardments and of making cannons; that he could build ships as well as armoured vehicles, catapults, and other war machines; and that he could execute sculpture in marble, bronze, and clay. He served as principal engineer in the duke's numerous military enterprises and was active also as an architect. In addition, he assisted the Italian mathematician Luca Pacioli in the celebrated work *Divina Proportione* (1509).

Evidence indicates that Leonardo had apprentices and pupils in Milan, for whom he probably wrote the various texts later compiled as *Treatise on Painting* (1651; translated 1956). The most important of his own paintings during the early Milan period was *The Virgin of the Rocks,* two versions of which exist (1483-1485, Louvre, Paris; 1490s to 1506-1508, National Gallery, London); he worked on the compositions for a long time, as was his custom, seemingly unwilling to finish what he had begun. From 1495 to 1497 Leonardo laboured on his masterpiece, *The Last Supper,* a mural in the refectory of the Monastery of Santa Maria delle Grazie, Milan. Unfortunately, his experimental use of oil on dry plaster (on what was the thin outer wall of a space designed for serving food) was technically unsound, and by 1500 its deterioration had begun. Since 1726 attempts have been made, unsuccessfully, to restore it; a concerted restoration and conservation program, making use of the latest technology, was begun in 1977 and is reversing some of the damage. Although much of the original surface is gone, the majesty of the composition and the penetrating characterization of the figures give a fleeting vision of its vanished splendour.

During his long stay in Milan, Leonardo also produced other paintings and drawings (most of which have been lost), theatre designs, architectural drawings, and models for the dome of Milan Cathedral. His largest commission was for a colossal bronze monument to Francesco Sforza, father of Ludovico, in the courtyard of Castello Sforzesco. In December 1499, however, the Sforza family was driven from Milan by French forces; Leonardo left the statue unfinished (it was destroyed by French archers, who used the terra cotta model as a target) and he returned to Florence in 1500.

In 1502 Leonardo entered the service of Cesare Borgia, duke of Romagna and son and chief general of Pope Alexander VI. In his capacity as the duke's chief architect and engineer, Leonardo supervised work on the fortresses of the papal territories in central Italy. In 1503 he was a member of a commission of artists who were to decide on the proper location for the *David* (1501-1504, Accademia, Florence), the famous colossal marble statue by the Italian sculptor Michelangelo, and he also served as an engineer in the war against Pisa. Toward the end of the year Leonardo began to design a decoration for the great hall of the Palazzo Vecchio. The subject was the Battle of Anghiari, a Florentine victory in its war with Pisa. He made many drawings for the decoration and completed a full-size cartoon, or sketch, in 1505, but he never finished the wall painting. The cartoon itself was destroyed in the 17th century, and the composition survives only in copies, of which the most famous is the one by the Flemish painter Peter Paul Rubens (1615, Louvre).

During this second Florentine period, Leonardo painted several portraits, but the only one that survives is the famous *Mona Lisa* (1503-1506, Louvre). One of the most celebrated portraits ever painted, it is also known as *La Gioconda,* after the presumed name of the woman's husband. Leonardo seems to have had a special affection for the picture, for he took it with him on all of his subsequent travels.

In 1506 Leonardo again went to Milan, at the summons of its French governor, Charles d'Amboise. The following year he was named court painter to King Louis XII of France, who was then residing in Milan. For the next six years Leonardo divided his time between Milan and Florence, where he often visited his half brothers and half sisters and looked after his inheritance. In Milan he continued his engineering projects and worked on an equestrian figure for a monument to Gian Giacomo Trivulzio, commander of the French forces in the city; although the project was not completed, drawings and studies have been preserved. From 1514 to 1516 Leonardo lived in Rome under the patronage of Pope Leo X. He was housed in the Palazzo Belvedere in the Vatican and seems to have been occupied principally with scientific experimentation. In 1516 he travelled to France to enter the service of King Francis I. He spent his last years at the Château de Cloux, near Amboise, where he died.

Although Leonardo produced a relatively small number of paintings, many of which remained unfinished, he was nevertheless an extraordinarily innovative and influential artist. During his early years, his style closely paralleled that of Verrocchio, but he gradually moved away from his teacher's stiff, tight, and somewhat rigid treatment of figures to develop a more evocative and atmospheric handling of composition. The early painting *The Adoration of the Magi* introduced a new approach to composition, in which the main figures are grouped in the foreground, while the background consists of distant views of imaginary ruins and battle scenes.

Leonardo's stylistic innovations are even more apparent in *The Last Supper,* in which he represented a traditional theme in an entirely new way. Instead of showing the 12 apostles as individual figures, he grouped them in dynamic compositional units of three, framing the figure of Christ, who is isolated in the center of the picture. Seated before a pale distant landscape seen through a rectangular opening in the wall, Christ—who is about to announce that one of those present will betray him—represents a calm nucleus while the others respond with animated gestures. In the monumentality of the scene and the weightiness of the figures,

Leonardo reintroduced a style pioneered more than a generation earlier by Masaccio, the father of Florentine painting. A 22-year project to remove accumulated dust and grease as well as earlier repainting from the mural was completed in 1999.

The *Mona Lisa,* Leonardo's most famous work, is as well-known for its mastery of technical innovations as for the mysteriousness of its legendary smiling subject. This work is a consummate example of two techniques—sfumato and chiaroscuro—of which Leonardo was one of the first great masters. Sfumato is characterized by subtle, almost infinitesimal transitions between colour areas, creating a delicately atmospheric haze or smoky effect; it is especially evident in the delicate gauzy robes worn by the sitter and in her enigmatic smile. Chiaroscuro is the technique of modeling and defining forms through contrasts of light and shadow; the sensitive hands of the sitter are portrayed with a luminous modulation of light and shade, while color contrast is used only sparingly.

Leonardo was among the first to introduce aerial perspective into his landscape backgrounds, an especially notable characteristic of his paintings. The chief masters of the High Renaissance in Florence, including Raphael, Andrea del Sarto, and Fra Bartolommeo, all learned from Leonardo; he completely transformed the school of Milan; and at Parma, the artistic development of Correggio was given direction by Leonardo's work.

Leonardo's many extant drawings, which reveal his brilliant draftsmanship and his mastery of the anatomy of humans, animals, and plant life, may be found in the principal European collections. The largest group is at Windsor Castle in England. Probably his most famous drawing is the magnificent self-portrait in old age (1510-1513, Biblioteca Reale, Turin, Italy).

Because none of Leonardo's sculptural projects was brought to completion, his approach to three-dimensional art can only be judged from his drawings. The same strictures apply to his architecture: None of his building projects was actually carried out as he devised them. In his architectural drawings, however, he demonstrates mastery in the use of massive forms, a clarity of expression, and especially a deep understanding of ancient Roman sources.

As a scientist Leonardo towered above all his contemporaries. His scientific theories, like his artistic innovations, were based on careful observation and precise documentation. He understood, better than anyone of his century or the next, the importance of precise scientific observation. Unfortunately, just as he frequently failed to bring to conclusion artistic projects, he never completed his planned treatises on a variety of scientific subjects. His theories are contained in numerous notebooks, most of which were written in mirror script. Because they were not easily decipherable, Leonardo's findings were not disseminated in his own lifetime; had they been published, they would have revolutionized the science of the 16th century. Leonardo actually anticipated many discoveries of modern times. In anatomy he studied the circulation of the blood and the action of the eye. He made discoveries in meteorology and geology, learned the effect of the moon on the tides, foreshadowed modern conceptions of continent formation, and surmised the nature of fossil shells. He was among the originators of the science of hydraulics and probably devised the hydrometer; his scheme for the canalization of rivers still has practical value. He invented a large number of ingenious machines, many potentially useful, among them an underwater diving suit. His flying devices, although not practicable, embodied sound principles of aerodynamics.

Famous Work: *Mona Lisa.*

❋❋

Albrecht Dürer

Albrecht Dürer (1471-1528), the most famous artist of Reformation Germany, widely known for his paintings, drawings, prints, and theoretical writings on art, all of which had a profound influence on 16th-century artists in his own country and in the Lowlands.

Dürer was born May 21, 1471, in Nürnberg. His father, Albrecht Dürer the Elder, was a goldsmith and his son's first art teacher. From his early training, the young Dürer inherited a legacy of 15th-century German art strongly dominated by Flemish late Gothic painting. German artists had little difficulty in adapting their own Gothic tradition to the Flemish art of Robert Campin, Jan van Eyck, and especially Rogier van der Weyden. The northern empirical (derived from observation rather than theory) approach to reality was their common bond. During the 16th century, stronger ties with Italy through trade, and the spread of Italian humanist ideas northward, infused the more conservative tradition of German art with new artistic ideas.

German artists found it difficult to reconcile their medieval devotional imagery—represented with rich textures, brilliant colours, and highly detailed figures—with the emphasis by Italian artists on the antique, on mythological subjects, and on idealized figures. Dürer's self-appointed task was to provide a model for his northern contemporaries by which they could combine their own empirical interest in naturalistic detail with the more theoretical aspects of Italian art. In his many letters—especially those to his lifelong friend, the humanist Willibald Pirckheimer—and in his various publications, Dürer stressed geometry and measurement as the keys to understanding the art of the Italian Renaissance and, through it, classical art. From about 1507 until his death, he made notes and drawings for his best-known treatise, the *Four Books on Human Proportions* (published posthumously, 1528). Artists of his day, however, more visually oriented than literary figures, looked more to Dürer's engravings and woodcuts than to his writings to guide them in their attempts to modernize their art with the classicizing nudes and idealized subjects of the Italian Renaissance.

After studying with his father, Dürer was apprenticed in 1486 to the painter and printmaker Michael Wolgemut at the age of 15. Between 1488 and 1493, Wolgemut's shop was engaged in the sizable task of providing numerous woodcut illustrations for the *Nürnberg Chronicle* (1493), by Hartmann Schedel, and Dürer must have received extensive instruction in making drawings for woodcut designs. Throughout the Renaissance, southern Germany was a center for publishing, and it was commonplace for painters of the period to be equally skilled at making woodcuts and engravings. As was customary for young men who finished their apprenticeships, Dürer embarked on his bachelor's journey in 1490. In 1492 he was in Colmar, where he tried to join the workshop of the German painter and engraver Martin Schongauer, who, unbeknownst to Dürer, had died in 1491. Dürer was advised by Schongauer's brothers to travel to the Swiss publishing center of Basel to find work. In Basel and later in Strasbourg, Dürer made illustrations for several publications, including Sebastian Brant's *Das Narrenschiff* (*Ship of Fools,* translated 1507) in 1494. During this early period of his life, between his apprenticeship and his return to Nürnberg in 1494, Dürer's art demonstrates his extreme facility with line and his keen observation of detail. These qualities are especially evident in a series of self-portraits, including an early drawing (1484, Albertina, Vienna) done when he was 13, a thoughtful portrait drawn in 1491 (University Collections, Erlangen, Germany), and a painting of himself as an extremely confident young man (1493, Louvre, Paris).

After marrying Agnes Frey in Nürnberg in 1494, he left for Italy. He produced some superbly detailed watercolour landscape studies, probably during his return journey—for example, a view of the Castle at Trent (National Gallery, London). During the next ten years in Nürnberg, from 1495 to 1505, Dürer produced a large number of works that firmly established his fame. These include his woodcut series the *Apocalypse* (1498) and the engravings *Large Fortune* (1501-1502) and *Adam and Eve* (1504). Collectively these works and others of the period show his increasing technical mastery of the woodcut and engraving media, his understanding of human proportions based on passages by the ancient Roman writer Vitruvius, and his brilliant ability to incorporate the details of nature into believable pictures of reality. His *Self-Portrait* of 1500 (Alte Pinakothek, Munich), in which he portrayed himself as a Christ-like figure, summarizes in visual form his lifelong concern for the elevation of the artist's status above that of a mere artisan.

Between 1505 and 1507, Dürer once again travelled to Italy. In Venice he met the great master Giovanni Bellini and other artists, and he obtained an important commission for a painting, the *Madonna of the Rose Garlands* (1506, National Museum, Prague), for the German Merchants' Foundation. Back in Nürnberg in 1507, he began a second period of great productivity in which he created such works as an altarpiece (1508-1509, destroyed by fire in 1729) for the Dominican church in Frankfurt; an *Adoration of the Trinity* panel (1508-1511, Kunsthistorisches Museum, Vienna); portraits; and many prints, including two editions of the *Passion,* woodcuts for *Triumphal Arch* for Holy Roman Emperor Maximilian I, and a series of engravings that included the *Knight, Death, and the Devil* (1513), *Saint Jerome in His Study* (1514), and *Melencolia I* (1514). Through the linear technique of engraving, Dürer was able to create tones of varying darkness and he used them to describe three-dimensional form.

In 1520, Dürer learned that Charles V, Maximilian's successor, was scheduled to travel to Aachen from Spain to be crowned Holy Roman emperor of the Habsburg dynasty. Dürer had received an annual stipend from Maximilian, and he was anxious to meet with Charles to have it continued. Armed with prints and other artworks, which he sold along the way to finance his trip, Dürer journeyed to Aachen and on to the Lowlands between 1520 and 1521. His diary provides a fascinating account of his travels, his audiences with royalty, and receptions by fellow artists, especially in Antwerp. His audience with Charles proved successful. He returned to Nürnberg, where he remained until his death on April 6, 1528. His last monumental works are two large panels, depicting the *Four Apostles* (1526, Alte Pinakothek), presented originally as his gift to the city of Nürnberg.

The quality of Dürer's work, his prodigious output, and his influence on his contemporaries all underscore the importance of his position in the history of art. In a broader context, his interest in geometry and mathematical proportions, his keen sense of history, his observations of nature, and his awareness of his own individual potential demonstrate the intellectually inquiring spirit of the Renaissance.

Famous Work: *Four Apostles.*

❊❊

Michelangelo

Michelangelo (1475-1564), Italian painter, sculptor, architect, and poet whose artistic accomplishments exerted a tremendous influence on his contemporaries and on subsequent European art. Michelangelo considered the male nude to be the foremost subject in art, and he explored its range of movement and expression in every medium. Even his architecture has a human aspect to it, in which a door, window, or support may refer to the face or body, or the position of architectural elements may suggest muscular tension.

Michelangelo continually sought challenge, whether physical, artistic, or intellectual. He favoured media that required hard physical labour—marble carving and fresco painting. In painting figures, he chose poses that were especially difficult to draw. And he gave his works several layers of meaning, by including multiple references to mythology, religion, and other subjects. His success in conquering the difficulties he set for himself is remarkable, but he left many of his works unfinished, as if he were defeated by his own ambition.

Michelangelo Buonarroti was born in the small village of Caprese and grew up in Florence. Florence was the artistic center of the early Renaissance, a period of outstanding artistic innovation and accomplishment that began in the early 1400s. In many ways the masterpieces that surrounded Michelangelo were his best teachers—ancient Greek and Roman statuary, and the paintings, sculpture, and architecture of early Renaissance masters Masaccio, Lorenzo Ghiberti, Donatello, Jacopo della Quercia, and Filippo Brunelleschi. As a child he preferred drawing to his schoolwork, despite his father's stern disapproval.

Eventually his father relented and allowed 13-year old Michelangelo to be apprenticed to Florentine painter Domenico

Ghirlandaio. Michelangelo's time in Ghirlandaio's workshop was marked with conflict, and his training there ended after only a year. Although he later denied that Ghirlandaio had any influence on him, he surely learned the technique of fresco painting from him, and his early drawings show some evidence of drawing methods used by Ghirlandaio.

From 1490 to 1492 Michelangelo lived in the house of Lorenzo de' Medici (known as Lorenzo the Magnificent), the then leading art patron of Florence. The Medici household was a gathering place for artists, philosophers, and poets. During this time Michelangelo met and perhaps studied with Bertoldo di Giovanni, an aging master who had trained with Donatello, the greatest sculptor of 15th-century Florence. Other members of the Medici circle inspired in Michelangelo a love of literature that he would develop in his poetry (a significant, if less-accomplished art form for him). They also taught him the ideas of Neoplatonism—a philosophy that regards the body as a trap for a soul that longs to return to God. Scholars interpret many of Michelangelo's works in terms of these ideas, in particular, his human figures that appear to break free from the stone that imprisons them.

Lorenzo de' Medici wished to revive the art of sculpture in the classical manner of the ancient Greeks and Romans, and he had a collection of ancient art that Michelangelo doubtless studied. Classical art provided an inspiration and a standard of excellence that Michelangelo hoped to surpass. Some of his earliest sculptures imitated classical works so closely that they were passed off as Roman originals. Later, Michelangelo was on hand in Rome for the excavation of a massive ancient sculpture of *Laocoön* (probably a Roman copy of a Greek original from the 2nd century BC, Vatican Museums, Vatican City). This powerful grouping of the Trojan prince Laocoön and his two sons, as they struggle to free themselves from huge snakes, provided a model of tense and twisting bodies that Michelangelo used in many of his late works, including the *Last Judgment* (1536-1541, Sistine Chapel, Vatican City).

Michelangelo was a very religious man, but he expressed his personal beliefs most clearly in his late works. His late drawings are introspective meditations on Christian themes such as the crucifixion, and in some works he inserted his own image as an onlooker in a religious scene.

Throughout his career Michelangelo came in contact with learned and powerful men. His patrons were wealthy businessmen, civic leaders, and church officials, including popes Julius II, Clement VII (born Giulio de' Medici, nephew of Lorenzo), and Paul III. Michelangelo strove to be accepted among his patrons as a gentleman, producing a large body of poetry and constructing a myth of noble ancestry. At the same time, he seemed to take pride in the physical work of making art. For example, he preferred the dirty and exhausting art of marble carving to that of panel painting, which he saw as something one could do in fine clothing. This is one of many contradictions in his life, but it is also an indication of the changing status of the artist—from craftsman to genius—that Michelangelo himself helped to bring about.

After political events led to the expulsion of the powerful Medici family from Florence in 1494, Michelangelo travelled to Venice, Bologna, and finally to Rome. He produced his first large-scale sculpture in Rome, a larger-than-life-size figure of a drunken *Bacchus* (1496-1498, Museo Nazionale, Bargello, Florence), the Roman god of wine. This sensual, nude youth is one of his few works of pagan rather than Christian subject matter and was based on ancient Greek and Roman statuary.

Pietà

One of Michelangelo's most memorable early works is a *Pietà* (1497-1500, St. Peter's Basilica, Vatican City). The Pietà theme shows Christ in his mother's lap, just after he is taken down from the cross. The theme was popular in France and northern Europe. But the two figures typically appeared awkward in northern art, with the body of a grown man lying stiffly across the lap of a much smaller woman, and with the wounds of Christ exaggerated to elicit a strong emotional response from the viewer. In contrast, Michelangelo's version shows Mary grieving silently and makes Christ's wounds barely visible. For intense emotionalism, Michelangelo substituted restrained but eloquent gestures—the Virgin calls our attention to her dead son with her left hand, while her right arm embraces him gently, lifting his arm slightly so that it hangs lifelessly before us. Mary's full robe forms a broad base for Christ's limp body, which curves slightly to wrap around hers, making the group graceful and compact.

Michelangelo originally intended for the piece to be placed within a shallow niche, and accordingly, he polished to a smooth finish all the surfaces that would have been visible and gave meticulous care to the drapery. This high degree of finish is rarely present in Michelangelo's work, and so probably reflects the tastes of the patron, a French cardinal who had commissioned the sculpture to be placed on his tomb. Michelangelo returned to the theme of the Pietà late in his life, in two of his most personal expressions: the Florentine *Pietà* (1547-1555, Museo dell'Opera del Duomo, Florence), which he meant to have placed on his own tomb, and the *Rondanini Pietà* (1555-1564, Castello Sforzesco, Milan), a work that remained unfinished when he died.

David

Michelangelo returned to Florence in 1501 to work on *David* (1501-1504, Galleria dell'Accademia, Florence). The subject of this work is the Old Testament story of David and Goliath, in which the young David, future king of Israel, flings a stone from his slingshot to kill the giant Goliath, thereby saving his nation. The statue expresses not only the daring of the young hero, but also of Michelangelo himself, who established himself as a master with this work. This massive statue, which stands 5.17 meters (17 ft) tall, was carved from a block of stone that another sculptor had left unfinished. Michelangelo drew on the classical tradition in depicting David as a nude, standing with his weight on one leg, the other leg at rest. This pose suggests impending movement, and the entire sculpture shows tense waiting, as David sizes up his enemy and considers his course of action.

While *David* reveals Michelangelo's expert knowledge of anatomy (he had been dissecting corpses for about five years), the head and hands are much too large in comparison with the torso. Critics have suggested several reasons for this inconsistency, but the most convincing is that the statue was originally intended for the roof of the Florence Cathedral, and exaggerating the head and hands made them more visible from a distance. The statue was never placed there, but set instead in front of the Palazzo della Signoria, the center of government in Florence. As a result its meaning changed: Rather than a religious image (it would have been one of several Old Testament figures on the cathedral), it became a symbol of the political strength of Florence against the forces of tyranny.

The Tomb of Julius II

In 1505 Michelangelo began work on a tomb for Pope Julius II that was to have stood in the apse of Saint Peter's Basilica in Rome. Michelangelo's earliest designs specify a freestanding structure with three levels: at the bottom, figures representing victory alternating with slaves; above them, four huge seated figures including Moses and Saint Paul; and finally, angels supporting either a coffin or an image of the pope. In all there would have been about 40 figures on a structure nearly as tall as a three-story building. But the scope of the work was drastically reduced as other projects delayed its completion.

In the end only three figures by Michelangelo's hand were placed on the tomb, which is now in Rome's church of San Pietro in Vincoli. Of these, the most powerful figure is *Moses* (about 1515), a dynamic example of Michelangelo's ability to infuse stone with a sense of movement and life. The muscular torso of Moses twists to the left, but his scowling face turns sharply to the right as if he has just seen the people worshiping their false god. His left leg is drawn back, as if he were about to rise to his feet in anger.

Two of the slave statues originally planned for the tomb, the *Rebellious Slave* and the *Dying Slave* (both about 1513-1516, Louvre, Paris, France), were also completed. They demonstrate Michelangelo's approach to carving, in which cutting away excess stone appears to release an entrapped human figure. Here, as in many of his sculptures, Michelangelo left parts of the block of stone rough and unfinished, either because he was satisfied with the statues as they were or because he no longer planned to use them.

Sistine Ceiling

A major project preventing completion of the tomb of Julius II was a new commission from Julius himself, to paint the ceiling of the Sistine Chapel in Rome. Between 1508 and 1512 Michelangelo created some of the most memorable images of all time on the vaulted ceiling of the papal chapel in the Vatican. His intricate system of decoration tells the biblical story of Genesis, beginning with God separating light and dark (above the altar), progressing to the story of Adam and Eve, and concluding with the story of Noah. Scenes from the biblical stories of David, Judith, Esther, and Moses are depicted in the corners, while images of prophets, *sibyls* (female prophets), and the ancestors of Christ are set in a painted architectural framework above the windows. Bright, clear colours enliven and unify the vast surface, and make the details more legible from the floor of the chapel.

The Creation of Adam from the Sistine Ceiling (1508-1512) is perhaps Michelangelo's finest fusion of form and meaning. Adam's pose echoes both the shape of the ground on which he reclines and the pose of God the Father, thus giving visual form to the biblical description of Adam as made from the earth in the likeness of God. We see Adam beginning to come to life, as he reaches listlessly toward the vigorous energy that the image of God embodies.

Church of San Lorenzo

The Tomb of Julius II required architectural planning, but Michelangelo's activity as an architect began in earnest with plan for the facade of the Church of San Lorenzo in Florence (designed 1516-1520, but never executed). Michelangelo probably had no formal training as an architect, but during the Renaissance it was not unusual for artists to be given architectural commissions simply because they had demonstrated the ability to draw and create designs. Michelangelo envisioned the San Lorenzo facade as a two-story marble screen supporting as many as 40 statues.

By 1520 funding was discontinued for the San Lorenzo facade, but Michelangelo remained occupied with other projects for this church. The commission for a sacristy (1519-1534) for San Lorenzo included plans for Medici family tombs. As did many of Michelangelo's designs, this one went through numerous changes before it was executed, but in the end it consisted of two large wall tombs facing each other across a high, domed room. One was intended for Giuliano de' Medici (duke of Nemours), the son of Lorenzo the Magnificent; the other for Giuliano's nephew Lorenzo (di Piero) de' Medici (duke of Urbino). Michelangelo conceived of the two tombs as representing opposite types: Giuliano symbolized the active, extroverted personality, Lorenzo, the contemplative, introspective one. He placed nudes representing *Day* and *Night* beneath *Giuliano*; nudes representing *Dawn* and *Dusk* beneath a seated *Lorenzo*. Plans for reclining river gods at the base of each tomb were never executed.

The elegant Laurentian Library (designed 1524-1534), adjoining the Church of San Lorenzo, confirmed Michelangelo's architectural abilities. In this and subsequent architectural projects, he combined classical motifs–columns, pediments, niches, and brackets—in new ways and distorted their relative proportions to give his architecture the surging energy of his sculpture and painting. In the entrance hall of the library, he invented new forms for the capitals of columns and tapered the *pilasters* (flattened pillars attached to walls) downward instead of upward. The curving contours of the central staircase seem to flow downward and outward, while rectilinear steps to its sides maintain a steady, upward march, giving a sense of checked energy.

The Last Judgment

Michelangelo was again called to work in the Sistine Chapel in 1534, when Clement VII (born Giulio de' Medici, nephew of Lorenzo the Magnificent) commissioned him to paint the wall above the altar. The *Last Judgment* (1536-1541), with which Michelangelo covered the wall, depicts Christ's second coming at the end of the world. The enormous scene is focused on the impassive figure of Christ whose right arm is poised to strike down the damned, while the left arm seems gently to call the blessed toward him. At his side is the Virgin Mary, traditionally included as a figure of mercy at the Last Judgment; she quietly looks downward toward those who emerge from their graves. The nude bodies of the saints and the figures rising to heaven are massive, perhaps to emphasize the belief that their physical bodies would be revived in a glorified state. The scene of hell in the lower right corner does not show Satan or various hellish torments as was customary, but is based instead on the *Inferno,* part of an early 14th-century epic poem, *The Divine Comedy,* by Italian writer Dante Alighieri. This and many other aspects of the *Last Judgment* (especially the nudity) were sharply criticized soon after the fresco was unveiled and helped it become one of the most talked about and most frequently copied works of art in the 16th century.

Piazza Del Campidoglio

Michelangelo's designs for the Piazza del Campidoglio (begun 1539, completed later by others) and its surrounding buildings succeeded in restoring this public space to its former role as the civic and political heart of Rome. Michelangelo's program for remodeling the *Campidoglio* (Italian for "capitol") began with a commission to create a new base for an ancient Roman bronze statue of emperor Marcus Aurelius on horseback. His plans soon expanded to include the addition of a double staircase to the building behind the statue, Palazzo Senatorio (completed 1544-1552); new and identical facades for the buildings to the sculpture's right and left, the Palazzo dei Conservatori (1563-1584) and the Palazzo Nuovo (1603-1650s); and finally a broad, ramplike stairway defines the uphill approach to the piazza.

The oval base Michelangelo designed for the statue of Marcus Aurelius became the basis for his design of the entire space. He placed the statue at the center of the piazza, which was paved in an oval pattern of radiating and interlocking lines. Approaching the piazza from the steps below, visitors are drawn into the receding space created by twin palaces, which angle subtly outward, and toward the staircase at either side of the Palazzo Senatorio. Perfect symmetry combines with flowing curves, traditional Roman forms with inventive new ones, to produce a unified and dynamic public space.

Saint Peter's Basilica

In 1546 Michelangelo was given the task of completing the design for Saint Peter's Basilica in the Vatican. Pope Julius II first gave the commission to Michelangelo's rival, Donato Bramante, in 1506. Bramante envisioned a church based upon a *Greek cross* (a cross with all four arms of equal length) and surmounted by a great dome. When Bramante died in 1514, only the enormous supports for the dome were in place, but these determined the scale and other elements of the design. At least three other architects contributed to the design before Michelangelo took over, with the most recent one having added a long nave to the church. Michelangelo returned to Bramante's plan, but made it more compact, strengthening the supports and unifying the exterior with gigantic pairs of pilasters with Corinthian capitals. The pilasters alternate with large openings topped with *pediments* (triangular forms). Around the base of the dome the line of the pilasters is echoed by fully rounded columns, which are in turn repeated on a smaller scale in the lantern at the top of the dome. The effect is one of great mass pushing upward, the forms varied in complex ways yet unified as a whole.

Drawings

Throughout his life, Michelangelo produced drawings of all sorts, including quick pen sketches, composition drawings, careful studies of anatomy, and architectural plans and elevations. In a special category, however, are the highly finished presentation drawings, meant to be seen as complete works of art and given as gifts to his closest friends. Some of these drawings represent classical myths, but he selected these myths and sometimes reshaped them to reflect personal meanings or to express Neoplatonic ideas. Others represent idealized human beings. An example is the *Divine Head* (1530, British Museum, London), a drawing of a female paired with the male *Count of Canossa* (original drawing lost). Using short strokes of chalk that are precisely *modulated* (varied in tone) and *stippling* (dots or flecks), Michelangelo creates an image of perfection. These are imaginative works, showing the skill of the artist both in the meticulous rendering of surfaces and in the wildly creative hairstyles or helmets he gives them.

Michelangelo's influence on his contemporaries and on later artists was profound. Mannerism was an art movement based on exaggeration of aspects of the style of Michelangelo and other artists of the late Renaissance. The mannerists were particularly drawn to the complex poses and elongated elegance of some of his figures. Later artists, including Annibale Carracci and Peter Paul Rubens, emulated the powerful strength of his figures but combined it with the graceful line of Raphael or the colours used by Titian, two of Michelangelo's contemporaries. But perhaps Michelangelo's greatest legacy to later artists is the image of the genius that he and those around him fashioned. Brooding, isolated, challenging, temperamental—these are the words that described Michelangelo's character and that we still use to describe artists seized by an inspiration that seems more than human.

Famous Work: *Sistine chapel ceiling.*

❋❋

Raphael

Raphael (painter) (1483-1520), Italian Renaissance painter, considered one of the greatest and most popular artists of all time.

Raphael was born Raffaello Santi or Raffaello Sanzio in Urbino on April 6, 1483, and received his early training in art from his father, the painter Giovanni Santi. According to many art historians, he also studied with Timoteo Viti at Urbino, executing under his influence a number of works of miniature-like delicacy and poetic atmosphere, including *Apollo and Marsyas* (Louvre, Paris) and *The Knight's Dream* (1501, National Gallery, London). In 1499 he went to Perugia, in Umbria, and became a student and assistant of the painter Perugino. Raphael imitated his master closely; their paintings of this period are executed in styles so similar that art historians have found it difficult to determine which were painted by Raphael. Among Raphael's independent works executed at Perugia are two large-scale paintings, the celebrated *Sposalizio,* or *Marriage of the Virgin* (1504, Brera Gallery, Milan), and *The Crucified Christ with the Virgin Mary, Saints and Angels* (1503, National Gallery, London).

In 1504 Raphael moved to Florence, where he studied the work of such established painters of the time as Leonardo da Vinci,

Michelangelo, and Fra Bartolommeo, learning their methods of representing the play of light and shade, anatomy, and dramatic action. At this time he made a transition from the typical style of the Umbrian school, with its emphasis on perspective and rigidly geometrical composition, to a more animated, informal manner of painting. His development during his Florentine period can best be traced in his numerous Madonnas. The earliest example, still Umbrian in inspiration, is the *Madonna del Granduca* (1504-1505, Pitti Palace, Florence). Later examples, showing the influence of Leonardo in serenity of expression and composition, include the well-known *La Belle Jardinière* (1507-1508, Louvre) and the *Madonna of the Goldfinch* (1505, Uffizi Gallery, Florence). The last of his Madonnas executed at Florence, the *Madonna del Baldacchino* (1508, Pitti Palace), a monumental altarpiece, is similar in style to the work of Fra Bartolommeo.

Raphael's most important commissions during his stay in Florence came from Umbria. His most original composition of this period is the *Entombment of Christ* (1507, Borghese Gallery, Rome), an altarpiece that nevertheless shows the strong influence of Michelangelo in the postures and anatomical development of the figures.

In 1508 Raphael was called to Rome by Pope Julius II and commissioned to execute frescoes in four small *stanze,* or rooms, of the Vatican Palace. The walls of the first room, the Stanza della Segnatura (1509-1511), are decorated with scenes elaborating ideas suggested by personifications of Theology, Philosophy, Poetry, and Justice, which appear on the ceiling. On the wall under Theology is the *Disputà,* representing a group discussing the mystery of the Trinity. The famous fresco *The School of Athens,* on the wall beneath Philosophy, portrays an open architectural space in which Plato, Aristotle, and other ancient philosophers are engaged in discourse. On the wall under Poetry is the celebrated *Parnassus,* in which the Greek god Apollo appears surrounded by the Muses and the great poets. The second Vatican chamber, the Stanza d'Eliodoro (1512-1514), painted with the aid of Raphael's assistants, contains scenes representing the triumph of the Roman Catholic church over its enemies.

After the death of Pope Julius II in 1513, and the accession of Leo X, Raphael's influence and responsibilities increased. He was made chief architect of Saint Peter's Basilica in 1514, and a year later was appointed director of all the excavations of antiquities in and near Rome. Because of his many activities, only part of the third room of the Vatican Palace, the Stanza del Incendio (1514-1517), was painted by him, and he merely provided the designs for the fourth chamber, the Sala Constantina. During this period he also designed ten tapestries illustrating the acts of Christ's apostles for the Sistine Chapel; the cartoons, or drawings, for these are now in the Victoria and Albert Museum, London. Raphael also devised the architecture and decorations of the Chigi Chapel in the Church of Santa Maria del Popolo and the decorations of the Villa Farnesina, which include the *Triumph of Galatea* (1513).

In addition to these major undertakings, he executed a number of easel paintings, including a portrait of Julius II (1511-1512), a series of Madonnas, and the world-famous *Sistine Madonna* (1514, Gemäldegalerie, Dresden). Other religious paintings during this period include the *Transfiguration* (1517-1520, Vatican), completed posthumously by the most notable of Raphael's many followers, Giulio Romano. Raphael died in Rome on his 37th birthday, April 6, 1520.

Famous Work: *Madonna.*

❋❋

Hans Holbein, the Younger

Hans Holbein, the Younger (1497-1543), German artist, one of the most accomplished masters of Renaissance portraiture, and a designer of woodcuts, stained glass, and jewellery.

Holbein was born in Augsburg. At an early age he began to study painting with his father, Hans Holbein the Elder, a recognized artist in the Flemish tradition who was a skilled portraitist. By 1515 Holbein the Younger had established himself in Basel, Switzerland, as a book illustrator. He designed many title-page woodcuts and completed a series of pen-and-ink sketches for *The Praise of Folie* by the Dutch scholar Desiderius Erasmus.

During a trip to Italy in 1518, Holbein encountered the works of the Italian Renaissance painters Andrea Mantegna and Leonardo da Vinci. The impact of these and other artists on Holbein's work can be seen in the Renaissance modeling and composition in his early portrait *Erasmus of Rotterdam* (1523, Louvre, Paris) and in his renowned *Dead Christ* and the *Passion of Christ* (both Kunstmuseum, Basel) and the altarpiece *Madonna of Burgomaster Meyer* (Grand Ducal Palace, Darmstadt), all completed between 1519 and 1526. In each of these Holbein showed the greater freedom in draftsmanship and the richness of colour that characterize the work of the North Italian masters. In his religious works Holbein integrated this wealth of detail and colour with the dignity and severity of characterization appropriate to a religious subject.

In the period 1523 to about 1526 Holbein increased his reputation as a book illustrator by a series of drawings portraying the medieval allegorical theme the Dance of Death and by a series of woodcuts for the German translation of the Bible by Martin Luther. Regardless of Holbein's prestige, however, as the austere attitudes of the Reformation further permeated Swiss society, artistic patronage diminished, and he was forced to go to England to gain new commissions. Arriving in 1526 with letters of introduction from Erasmus, now his friend and patron, Holbein was engaged to portray several of the great humanists of the period, including Sir Thomas More.

Returning to Basel in 1528, Holbein was commissioned to make improvements in an earlier work, *Justice* (1521-1522), with which he had decorated the council chamber of the town hall. His additions to this series of frescoes reflect his continuing growth as an artist; the newer, less crowded compositions convey a still greater dramatic impact than his earlier scenes. Unfortunately, none of Holbein's many great frescoes executed here and in England and Germany have survived intact. Their beauty must be judged, instead, from his sketches and copies of the frescoes made by later artists. Holbein settled again in England in 1532 and began his career as a master portrait painter. His portrait of the statesman Thomas Cromwell brought the artist recognition at court, and by 1536 he was established as court painter to Henry VIII. His most significant works, the portraits of Henry VIII and his wife Jane Seymour, were destroyed by fire in 1698. Several of his portraits of other court figures, including most of Henry VIII's wives and his son Edward (later Edward VI), are still extant. The preliminary drawings for these paintings, in which Holbein combined chalk, silverpoint, pen, and other media, are among his most admired works. A group of 87 drawings is in the royal collection at Windsor Castle. Holbein died in London in 1543 during a plague epidemic.

Holbein's reputation is based on his realistic portrayals of individuals and groups. His attention to every detail of flesh, hair, dress, and ornamentation and his ability to capture their exact texture neither detract from nor betray the basic character and dignity of his subjects. Holbein also contributed many important drawings for the great Renaissance art of glass painting; he also painted miniatures.

Famous Work: *Sir Thomas More.*

**

El Greco

El Greco, (1541-1614), Spanish Mannerist painter, whose work, with that of Francisco de Goya and Diego Velázquez, represents the acme of Spanish art. El Greco (meaning "The Greek") was born in Candia, now Iráklion, Crete (Kríti) (then a possession of the Republic of Venice), in 1541 and was named Domenikos Theotokopoulos.Details of his early life and training are sketchy, but he probably first studied painting in his native city. Although no works from his first years survive, they were probably painted in the late Byzantine style popular in Crete at the time. Reminiscences of this style are seen in his later work. He was an erudite man, whose taste for classical and contemporaneous literature seems to have developed in his youth.

About 1566, El Greco went to Venice, where he remained until 1570. He was employed in the workshop of Titian and was also strongly influenced by Tintoretto, both masters of the High Renaissance. Such early Venetian paintings as his *Christ Healing the Blind Man* (1566-1567, Gemäldegalerie, Dresden) demonstrate his assimilation of Titianesque colour and of Tintoretto's figural compositions and use of deep spatial recesses. Further Italian inspiration came during the years El Greco spent in Rome, from 1570 to 1576. The sculptural qualities of the work of Italian artist Michelangelo inspired him, as is evident in his *Pietà* (1570-1572, Philadelphia Museum of Art) and *Purification of the Temple*

(1570-1575, Minneapolis Institute of Arts). A study of Roman architecture also reinforced the stability of his compositions, which often include views of Roman Renaissance buildings.

In Rome he met several Spaniards associated with the church in Toledo, who may have persuaded him to come to Spain. In 1576 he left Italy and, after a brief sojourn in Malta, arrived in Toledo in the spring of 1577. He quickly began work on his first Spanish commission, producing for the Church of Santo Domingo el Antiguo the sumptuous *Assumption of the Virgin* (1577, Art Institute of Chicago), a painting that marks a turning point in his art. Although compositionally based on Titian's *Assumption* (1516-1518) in Santa Maria dei Frari in Venice, the colours and spatial relationships are less Italianate. A move toward nonnormative colours, groupings, and figural proportions became more marked in El Greco's art with each successive phase.

El Greco was anxious to be given the commission to fresco the walls of the newly built royal monastery-palace of El Escorial near Madrid, completed in 1582. He submitted several paintings to King Philip II for approval but was denied the commission. One of these, *The Triumph of the Holy League* (1578-1579, versions in El Escorial and in the National Gallery, London), proves his ability to combine complex political iconography with medieval motifs. El Greco also worked for Toledo Cathedral: The *Disrobing of Christ* (1577-1579) for the sacristy presents a splendid image of Christ in a rich red garment, closely surrounded by his captors. The work caused the first of several lawsuits brought by the artist against his patrons, who objected to its high price.

In 1586 El Greco painted one of his greatest masterpieces, *The Burial of Count Orgaz,* for the Church of Santo Tomé in Toledo. This work, still in place, portrays a 14th-century Toledan nobleman laid in his grave (in actuality situated just below the painting) by Saints Stephen and Augustine. Above, the count's soul rises to a heaven densely populated with angels, saints, and contemporary political figures. *The Burial* also manifests El Greco's typical elongation of figures and a *horror vacui* (dread of unfilled spaces), features of his art that became more pronounced in later years. These characteristics may be associated with international Mannerism, which is still evident in the art of El Greco sometime after it had ceased to be widely popular in European painting. El Greco's intensely personal vision was rooted in his highly cultivated spirituality. Indeed, there is present in his canvases a mystical atmosphere similar to that evoked in the writings of such contemporaneous Spanish mystics as Saint Teresa of Ávila and Saint John of the Cross, although no evidence exists that El Greco had any personal contact with them.

El Greco was a prosperous man. He had a large house in Toledo, where he received members of the nobility and the intellectual elite, such as the poets Luis de Góngora and Fray Hortensio Felix de Paravicino, whose portrait, painted by El Greco from 1609 to 1610, is now in the Museum of Fine Arts, Boston. El Greco also painted views of the city of Toledo itself, such as *View of Toledo* (1600–1610, Metropolitan Museum of Art, New York City), even though landscape was a genre traditionally neglected by Spanish artists.

A feverish intensity can be sensed in many of El Greco's canvases dating from the 1590s until the time of his death. *Baptism of Christ* (signed in Greek, as was the artist's custom, 1596-1600) and *Adoration of the Shepherds* (1612-1614), both in the Prado, seem to pulsate with an eerie light generated by the holy figures themselves. In addition, the *Adoration* figures are enveloped by a steamy haze, observable in other late works, which intensifies the mystical nature of the event.

Subjects of classical mythology, such as the *Laocoön* (1610-1614, National Gallery, Washington, D.C.), and Old Testament history, such as the unfinished apocalyptic scene *Opening of the Fifth Seal* (1608-1614, Metropolitan Museum), attest to El Greco's humanistic learning and his brilliantly personal and novel approach to traditional themes. El Greco died in Toledo on April 7, 1614, and he was buried there in Santo Domingo el Antiguo.

Famous Work: *Burial of Count Orgaz.*

❋❋

Sir Peter Paul Rubens

Peter Paul Rubens, (1577-1640), Flemish painter, considered the most important of the 17th century, whose style came to define the animated, exuberantly sensuous aspects of baroque painting. Combining the bold brushwork, luminous colour, and shimmering light of the Venetian school with the vigor of the art of Michelangelo and the formal dynamism of Hellenistic sculpture, Rubens created a vibrant style, with an energy that emanates from tensions between the intellectual and the emotional, the classical and the romantic. For more than two centuries after his death, the vitality and eloquence of his work continued to influence such artists as Jean-Antoine Watteau in the early 18th century and Eugène Delacroix and Pierre Auguste Renoir in the 19th century.

Rubens's father, Jan Rubens, was a prominent lawyer and Antwerp alderman who converted from Catholicism to Calvinism. In 1568 he left Flanders with his family to escape persecutions against Protestants. Peter Paul was born in exile in Siegen, Westphalia (now in Germany), also the birthplace of his brother Philip and his sister Baldina. In Westphalia, Jan Rubens became the adviser and lover of Princess Anna of Saxony, wife of Prince William I of Orange (William the Silent).

When Jan Rubens died in 1587, his widow returned the family to Antwerp, where she and the children became Catholics. After studying the classics in a Latin school and serving as a court page, Peter Paul decided to become a painter. He apprenticed in turn with Tobias Verhaecht, Adam van Noort, and Otto van Veen, called Vaenius, three minor Flemish painters influenced by 16th-century Mannerist artists of the Florentine-Roman school. The young Rubens was as precocious a painter as he had been a scholar of modern European languages and classical antiquity. In 1598, at the age of 21, he was accorded the rank of master painter of the Antwerp Guild of Saint Luke.

Shortly thereafter, following the example of many northern European artists of the period, Rubens travelled to Italy, the center of European art for the previous two centuries. In 1600 he arrived in Venice, where he was particularly inspired by the paintings of Titian, Paolo Veronese, and Tintoretto. Later, while living in Rome, he was influenced by the works of Michelangelo and Raphael, as well as by ancient Greco-Roman sculpture.

Vincenzo Gonzaga, the duke of Mantua, employed Rubens for about nine years. Rubens copied Renaissance paintings for the ducal collection, but he was also able to execute original works. In 1605 he served as the duke's emissary to King Philip III of Spain.

During his years in Italy, Rubens was exposed to the early baroque works of contemporary Italian painters Annibale Carracci and Caravaggio, and he associated with some of the leading humanist intellectuals of the day. Gradually, the bourgeois Flemish painter became a gentleman artist of international repute.

It was news of his mother's impending death that brought Rubens back to Antwerp in 1608. Although he did not arrive in time to see his mother alive, he remained in Antwerp, where he married Isabella Brant the following year. While in Italy, Rubens had formulated one of the first innovative expressions of the baroque style, which on his return earned him recognition as the foremost painter of Flanders. He was immediately employed by the burgomaster of Antwerp. His success was further confirmed in 1609, when he was engaged as court painter to the Austrian archduke Albert and his wife, the Spanish infanta Isabella, who together ruled the Low Countries as viceroys for the king of Spain. The number of pictures requested from Rubens was so large that he established an enormous workshop, in which he would execute the initial sketch and final touches while his apprentices completed all the intermediary steps.

In addition to receiving court commissions from Brussels and abroad, the highly devout Rubens was much in demand by the militant Counter Reformation church of Flanders, which regarded his dramatic, emotionally charged interpretations of religious events—such as the *Triptych of the Raising of the Cross* (1610-1611, Antwerp Cathedral)—as effective instruments for spiritual recruitment and renewal. Prosperity allowed Rubens to build an Italianate residence in Antwerp, where he housed his extensive collection of art and antiquities.

Between 1622 and 1630 Rubens's role as a diplomat was equal to his importance as a painter. In 1622 he visited Paris, where the French queen Marie de Médicis commissioned him, for the Luxembourg Palace, to depict her life in a series of allegorical paintings, which he completed in 1625. Despite the keen loss Rubens felt after the death of his wife in 1626, he continued to be highly productive. In 1628 he was sent by the Flemish viceroys to Spain.

While in Madrid, he received several commissions from King Philip IV of Spain, who made him secretary of his Privy Council. Rubens also served as a mentor to the young Spanish painter Diego Velázquez. After a delicate diplomatic mission to London in 1629, Rubens was knighted by a grateful King Charles I of England, for whom he executed several paintings, as well as the preliminary sketches (finished in Antwerp, 1636) for the ceiling mural in the Whitehall Palace Banqueting Hall.

From 1630, when he married Hélène Fourment, until his death, Rubens remained in Antwerp, primarily at Castle Steen, his country residence. During the final decade of his life, he continued to execute commissions for the Habsburg monarchs of Austria and Spain. Increasingly, he also painted pictures of personal interest, especially of his wife and children and of the Flemish countryside.

The concerns of Rubens's late style, and indeed of his whole career, are summarized in *The Judgment of Paris* (1635, National Gallery, London). In this painting, the richness of creation is symbolized by the voluptuous goddesses and the verdant landscape against which they pose. Luxuriant colour, glowing light and shade, sensuous brushwork, and an elegant composition all serve to further the meaning of the narrative: Paris's selection of the most beautiful goddess.

Famous Work: *Descent from the Cross.*

❋❋

Rembrandt Van Rijn

Rembrandt (1606-1669), Dutch baroque artist, who ranks as one of the greatest painters in the history of Western art. His full name was Rembrandt Harmenszoon van Rijn. He possessed a profound understanding of human nature that was matched by a brilliant technique—not only in painting but in drawing and etching—and his work made an enormous impact on his contemporaries and influenced the style of many later artists. Perhaps no painter has ever equaled Rembrandt's chiaroscuro effects or his bold impasto.

Born in Leiden on July 15, 1606, Rembrandt was the son of a miller. Despite the fact that he came from a family of relatively modest means, his parents took great care with his education. Rembrandt began his studies at the Latin School, and at the age of 14 he was enrolled at the Leiden University. The program did not interest him, and he soon left to study art—first with a local master, Jacob van Swanenburch, and then, in Amsterdam, with Pieter Lastman, known for his historical paintings. After six months, having mastered everything he had been taught, Rembrandt returned to Leiden, where he was soon so highly regarded that although barely 22 years old, he took his first pupils, among them Gerrit Dou.

Rembrandt moved to Amsterdam in 1631; his marriage in 1634 to Saskia van Uylenburgh, the cousin of a successful art dealer, enhanced his career, bringing him in contact with wealthy patrons who eagerly commissioned portraits. An exceptionally fine example from this period is the *Portrait of Nicolaes Ruts* (1631, Frick Collection, New York City). In addition, Rembrandt's mythological and religious works were much in demand, and he painted numerous dramatic masterpieces such as *The Blinding of Samson* (1636, Städelsches Kunstinstitut, Frankfurt). Because of his renown as a teacher, his studio was filled with pupils, some of whom (such as Carel Fabritius) were already trained artists. In the 20th century, scholars have reattributed a number of his paintings to his associates; attributing and identifying Rembrandt's works is an active area of art scholarship.

In contrast to his successful public carrer, however, Rembrandt's family life was marked by misfortune. Between 1635 and 1641 Saskia gave birth to four children, but only the last, Titus, survived; her own death came in 1642. Hendrickje Stoffels, engaged as his housekeeper about 1649, eventually became his common-law wife and was the model for many of his pictures.

Despite Rembrandt's financial success as an artist, teacher, and art dealer, his penchant for ostentatious living forced him to declare bankruptcy in 1656. An inventory of his collection of art and antiquities, taken before an auction to pay his debts, showed the breadth of Rembrandt's interests: ancient sculpture, Flemish and Italian Renaissance paintings, Far Eastern art, contemporary Dutch works, weapons, and armour. Unfortunately, the results of the auction—including the sale of his house—were disappointing.

These problems in no way affected Rembrandt's work; if anything, his artistry increased. Some of the great paintings from this period are *The Jewish Bride* (1632), *The Syndics of the Cloth Guild* (1661, Rijksmuseum, Amsterdam), *Bathsheba* (1654, Louvre, Paris), *Jacob Blessing the Sons of Joseph* (1656, Staatliche Gemäldegalerie, Kassel, Germany), and a self-portrait (1658, Frick Collection). His personal life, however, continued to be marred by sorrow, for his beloved Hendrickje died in 1663, and his son, Titus, in 1668. Eleven months later, on October 4, 1669, Rembrandt died in Amsterdam.

Rembrandt may have created more than 600 paintings as well as an enormous number of drawings and etchings. The style of his earliest paintings, executed in the 1620s, shows the influence of his teacher, Pieter Lastman, in the choice of dramatic subjects, crowded compositional arrangements, and emphatic contrasts of light and shadow. *The Noble Slav* (1632, Metropolitan Museum of Art, New York City) shows Rembrandt's love of exotic costumes, a feature characteristic of many of his early works.

A magnificent canvas, *Portrait of a Man and His Wife* (1633, Isabella Stewart Gardner Museum, Boston), shows his early portrait style—his preoccupation with the sitters' features and with details of clothing and room furnishings; this careful rendering of interiors was to be eliminated in his later works. Members of Rembrandt's family who served as his models are sometimes portrayed in other guises, as in *Rembrandt's Mother as the Prophetess Anna* (1631, Rijksmuseum), or the wistful *Saskia as Flora,* (1634, the Hermitage, Saint Petersburg).

Perhaps no artist ever painted as many self-portraits (about 60), or subjected himself to such penetrating self-analysis. Not every early portrayal, however, can be interpreted as objective representation, for these pictures frequently served as studies of various emotions, later to be incorporated into his biblical and historical paintings. The self-portraits also may have served to demonstrate his command of chiaroscuro; thus, it is difficult to tell what Rembrandt looked like from such a self-portrait as the one painted about 1628 (Rijksmuseum, on loan from the Daan Cevat Collection, England), in which deep shadows cover most of his face, barely revealing his features. On the other hand, in none of these youthful self-portraits did he attempt to disguise his homely features.

Biblical subjects account for about one-third of Rembrandt's entire production. This was somewhat unusual in Protestant Holland of the 17th century, for church patronage was non-existent and religious art was not regarded as important. In Rembrandt's early biblical works, drama was emphasized, in keeping with baroque taste.

Amont Rembrand's first major public commissions in Amsterdam was the *Anatomy Lesson of Dr. Tulp* (1632, Mauritshuis, The Hague). This work depicts the regents of the Guild of Surgeons gathered for a dissection and lecture. Such group portraits were a genre unique to Holland and meant substantial income for an artist in a country where neither church nor royalty acted as patrons of art. Rembrandt's painting surpasses commemorative portraits made by other Dutch artists with its interesting pyramidal arrangement of the figures, lending naturalism to the scene.

Many of Rembrandt's paintings of the 1640s show the influence of classicism in style and spirit. A 1640 self-portrait (National Gallery, London), based on works by the Italian Renaissance artists Raphael and Titian, reflects his assimilation of classicism both in formal organization and in his expression of inner calm. In the *Portrait of the Mennonite Preacher Anslo and His Wife* (1641, Staatliche Museen, Berlin-Dahlem), quieter in feeling than his earlier work, the interplay between the figures is masterfully rendered; the preacher speaks, perhaps explaining a biblical passage to his wife, who quietly listens. A number of Rembrandt's other works depict dialogues and, like this one, represent one specific moment. In the moving *Supper at Emmaus* (1648, Louvre), Rembrandt's use of light immediately conveys the meaning of the scene.

His group portraiture continued to develop in richness and complexity. The so-called *Night Watch*—more accurately titled *The Shooting Company of Captain Frans Banning Cocq* (1642, Rijksmuseum)—portrays the bustling activity of a military company, gathered behind its leaders, preparing for a parade or shooting contest. In departing from the customary static mode of painting rows of figures for the corporate portrait, Rembrandt achieved a powerful dramatic effect. Despite the popular myth that the painting was rejected by those who commissioned it, and led to a decline in Rembrandt's reputation and fortune, it was actually well received.

Many of Rembrandt's landscapes in this middle period are romantic and based on his imagination rather than recording specific places. The inclusion of ancient ruins and rolling hills, not a part of the flat Dutch countryside, as in *River Valley with Ruins* (Staatliche Gemäldegalerie, Kassel), suggests a classical influence derived from Italy.

Rembrandt's greatest paintings were created during the last two decades of his life. Baroque drama, outward splendor, and superficial details no longer mattered to him. His self-portraits, portrayals of single figures and groups, and historical and religious works reveal a concern with mood and with spiritual qualities. His palette grew richly colouristic and his brushwork became increasingly bold; he built thick impastos that seem miraculously to float over the canvas. In *Portrait of the Painter in Old Age* (1669, National Gallery, London), Rembrandt's features betray a slightly sarcastic mood. One of his finest single portraits (1654, Stichting Jan Six, Amsterdam) is that of Jan Six. Six, wearing a deeply coloured red, gold, and gray costume, is shown putting on a glove. The portrait is painted in a semiabstract style that demonstrates Rembrandt's daring technical bravura. Six's quiet, meditative mood is expressed by the subtle play of light on his face. In such late biblical works as *Potiphar's Wife Accusing Joseph* (1655, Staatliche Museen, Berlin-Dahlem), and the very moving *Return of the Prodigal Son* (1669, the Hermitage) Rembrandt concentrated on the inherent psychological drama rather than on the excitement of the narrative as he had in works of his early period. In general, after his early period, Rembrandt was not particularly interested in allegorical and mythological subjects.

For Rembrandt, drawing and etching were as much major vehicles of expression as painting. Some 1400 drawings, recording a wide range of outward and inner visions, are attributed to him, works mostly done for their own sake rather than as preparatory studies for paintings or prints. The majority of them are not signed, because they were made for his private use. Rembrandt's early drawings (of the 1630s) were frequently executed in black or red chalk; later his favourite medium became pen and ink on white paper, often in combination with brushwork, lending a tonal accent. In some drawings, such as *The Finding of Moses* (1635, Rijksprentenkabinet, Amsterdam), a few charged lines indicating three figures carry maximum expression. Other drawings were, in contrast, highly finished, such as *The Eastern Gate at Rhenen* (*Oostpoort*) (1648, Musée, Bayonne, France), which displays details of architecture and perspective. He made masterful drawings throughout the early as well as mature phases of his career. An example of an early work is *Portrait of a Man in an Armchair, Seen Through a Frame* (1634, private collection, New York City), done in chalk, considered Rembrandt's most finished portrait drawing. Superb later works are *Nathan Admonishing David* (1655-1656, Metropolitan Museum), done with a reed pen, and a genre piece, *A Woman Sleeping* (*Hendrickje*) (1655, British Museum, London), a powerful brush drawing universally praised as one of his finest.

Rembrandt's etchings were internationally renowned even during his lifetime. He exploited the etching process for its unique potential, using scribbling strokes to produce extraordinarily expressive lines. In combination with etching he employed the drypoint needle, achieving special effects with the burr in his mature graphic work. Indeed, Rembrandt's most impressive etchings date from his mature period. They include the magnificent full-length portrait of Jan Six (1647, Bibliothèque Nationale, Paris), the famous *Christ Healing the Sick,* also known as the *100 Guilder Print* (1642-1645), the poetic landscape *Three Trees* (1643), and *Christ Preaching,* or *La Petite Tombe* (1652), all in the British Museum.

Famous Work: *The Night Watch.*

❊❊

Jan Vermeer

Jan Vermeer, (1632-1675), Dutch painter, who excelled in portraying interior scenes that are composed with mathematical precision and suffused with cool, silvery light. Vermeer, also called Jan van der Meer van Delft, was born in Delft. After serving an apprenticeship, he was admitted in 1653 to the guild of Saint Luke of Delft as a master painter. An important member of the guild, he served four terms on its board of governors and is believed to have been well-known to his contemporaries. He made a modest living as an art dealer rather than as a painter.

Only 35 of Vermeer's paintings have survived, although few of his paintings are believed to have disappeared: The number of extant works is close to the number of works for which some documentation exists. Their small number is the result of Vermeer's deliberate, methodical work habits and his comparatively short life. None of his paintings appear to have been sold during his lifetime, and at his death, in Delft, he left many debts to his impoverished wife and their 11 children. Little is known of Vermeer's life or working habits.

With a few exceptions, including some landscapes, street scenes, and portraits, Vermeer painted sunlit domestic interiors in which one or two figures are shown engaged in reading, writing, performing domestic tasks, or playing musical instruments. These objectively observed, precisely executed genre paintings of

17th-century Dutch life are characterized by a geometrical sense of order. The skewed perspective evident in some works (in which the nearest objects are disproportionately large) and the out-of-focus impression conveyed by sections of his paintings indicate that he may have experimented with a camera obscura, a precursor to the modern camera.

Vermeer was a master of composition and in the representation of space. He arranged neutral, muted hues over the foreground, into the middle ground, and farther into the distance to provide a natural perspective in such works as *Girl Asleep at a Table* (1656, Metropolitan Museum of Art, New York City). In *Maidservant Pouring Milk* (1660, Rijksmuseum, Amsterdam), *Woman with a Water Jug* (1663, Metropolitan Museum of Art), *View of Delft* (1660, Mauritshuis, The Hague), and other works, he recorded the effects of light with a subtlety, delicacy, and purity of colour that have probably never been surpassed. His other paintings include *Soldier and Laughing Girl* (1657, Frick Collection, New York City) and *Girl with a Red Hat* (1667, National Gallery of Art, Washington, D.C.).

After his death Vermeer did not receive attention until the late 19th century. His reputation steadily increased thereafter, and today he is considered one of the greatest Dutch painters. His work was forged in the early 20th century and sold to the Germans during World War II (1939-1945).

Famous Work: *Girl with a Pearl Earring.*

❋❋

Antonio Canaletto

Born Oct. 18, 1697, Venice [Italy] died April 20, 1768, Venice, byname *of Giovanni Antonio Canal* Italian topographical painter whose masterful expression of atmosphere in his detailed views (*vedute*) of Venice and London and English country homes influenced succeeding generations of landscape artists.

Canaletto was born into a noble family whose coat of arms he occasionally used as a signature. How he came to be known as Canaletto is uncertain, however; perhaps the name was first used to distinguish him from his father, Bernardo Canal, a theatrical scene painter in whose studio Canaletto assisted. Canaletto is recorded as working with his father and brother in Venice from 1716 to 1719 and in Rome in 1719–20, painting scenes for Alessandro Scarlatti operas. It was in Rome that Canaletto left theatrical painting for the topographical career that was to bring him international fame so quickly, although a close connection to his theatrical work remained in his choice of subject matter, his use of line and wash drawings, and his theatrical perspective.

When he returned to Venice, he began his contact with the foreign patrons who would continue as his chief support throughout his career. Four large paintings were completed for the Prince of Liechtenstein, in or before 1723, and in 1725–26 he finished a series of pictures for Stefano Conti, a merchant from Lucca. Dated memorandums accompanying the Conti pictures suggest how busy and yet how exacting the artist was at this time. Canaletto indicates that delays in the delivery of the pictures had been due to the pressure of other commissions and his own insistence on obtaining reliable pigments and on working from nature. In his pictures of the late 1720s, such as "*The Stonemason's Yard*", he combined a freedom and subtlety of manner that he was rarely to achieve again with an unrivaled imaginative and dramatic interpretation of Venetian architecture. His understanding of sunlight and shadow, cloud effects, and the play of light on buildings support the contention in his memorandums that he was working out-of-doors, which was a most unusual procedure for painters of that time.

Throughout the 1730s Canaletto was deeply absorbed in meeting foreign demands for souvenir views of Venice. Such was the pressure upon him that he ultimately was forced to work largely from drawings and even from other artists' engravings, rather than from nature. He also developed the use of the *camera ottica,* a device by which a lens threw onto a ground-glass screen the image of a view, which could be used as a basis for a drawing or painting. Finally, he developed a mechanical technique, in which ruler and compasses played a part, and architecture and figures were put into the picture according to a dexterous and effective formula. Such a vast number of views of Venice were produced during his lifetime that it is often thought that Canaletto was head of a large studio, but there is no evidence of this.

Canaletto had no serious rivals. The painter Luca Carlevaris, who may have been his initial inspiration in choosing to produce topographical pictures for a largely foreign audience, had been driven from the field; Bernardo Bellotto, Canaletto's nephew, was not yet a mature painter; and Michele Marieschi was a follower rather than a competitor. Because of this lack of rivals, Canaletto became increasingly difficult to deal with. Owen Mac Swinney, an English operatic figure and patron of Canaletto, wrote as early as 1727,

'The fellow is whimsical and varies his prices, every day: and he that has a mind to have any of his work, must not seem to be too fond of it, for he'l be ye worse treated for it, both in the price and the painting too'.

The outbreak of the War of the Austrian Succession in 1740, which cut down sharply the number of visitors to Venice, seriously affected Canaletto's commissions. At this point, an early acquaintance, Joseph Smith—publisher, merchant, and later British consul in Venice—stepped into the breach. As standardized views of Venice dropped from demand, Smith seems to have encouraged Canaletto to expand his range of subjects to include Roman monuments and the area of Padua and the Brenta River. Pictures composed of more or less recognizable elements rearranged (*capriccio*) and pictures composed of almost completely imaginary architectural and scenic elements (*veduta ideata*) now began to play an increasingly important part in Canaletto's work. In 1741–44 Canaletto also made a series of 30 etchings, exceptionally skillful and sensitive, showing a command of perspective and luminosity.

Canaletto's international reputation served him well as the tourists became more scarce. In 1746 he went to England, where he was welcomed, and remained until 1755, despite an invitation to Dresden from the elector of Saxony. He worked mainly in London, on English views. It is notable, when considering the works executed during this period, that Canaletto—an artist 50 years of age who had evolved various conventions based on Venetian experience–was dealing with an entirely different set of atmospheric conditions and different subject matter. Occasionally, by putting English material into a Venetian framework, he achieved a masterpiece, but for the most part he fell below his own standards, and his work was lifeless and mechanical.

On his return to Venice, however, his reputation had not diminished; and at last he received official recognition—election to the Venetian Academy in 1763 and, in the same year, appointment as prior of the Collegio dei Pittori.

Famous Work: *The Grand Canal and the Church of the Salute, Venice.*

❊❊

Sir Joshua Reynolds

Sir Joshua Reynolds, (1723-1792), English painter in the Grand Manner, who was the foremost portraitist of his day and one of the most important and influential figures in the history of English painting. Reynolds was born in Plympton, Devonshire, the son of a cleric and schoolmaster. He learned portraiture in London from the painter Thomas Hudson, and in 1749 he sailed to the Mediterranean with Commodore Augustus Keppel. After three years travelling in Italy he returned to London, where soon he attracted notice for his portraits of prominent figures. He came to be the first English painter to achieve social recognition and elevated status for his artistic achievements.

In 1764 Reynolds founded the Literary Club, which included essayist and critic Samuel Johnson, actor David Garrick, statesman Edmund Burke, writer Oliver Goldsmith, writer James Boswell, and dramatist Richard Brinsley Sheridan. When the Royal Academy of Arts was instituted in 1768, Reynolds was elected president and was knighted. In 1769 he delivered the first of his annual *Discourses* (published 1778) to the students of the academy, in which he set forth the idealistic, moralizing principles of academic art. In 1784 he succeeded Allan Ramsay as painter to the king. In the same year he exhibited his portrait of the English actor Sarah Siddons as the *Tragic Muse* (one version, 1784, Huntington Art Gallery, San Marino, California), probably his greatest portrait. Other well-known paintings are *Nelly O'Brien* (1760-1762, Wallace Collection, London), *Lady Sarah Bunbury Sacrificing to the Graces* (1765, Art Institute of Chicago), *Heads of Angels* (1787, Tate Gallery, London), and *Age of Innocence* (1788, Tate Gallery).

Reynolds is credited with more than 2000 portraits noted for their rich variety. Stylistically, he was influenced by Michelangelo and the Flemish painter Peter Paul Rubens. Reynolds's portraits are distinguished by calm dignity, classical allusions, rich colour, and realistic portrayal of character. Unfortunately, his use of bitumen (or asphalt) and experimental pigments made some of his colours fade prematurely.

Famous Work: *The Family of the Duke of Marlborough.*

❋❋

Thomas Gainsborough

Thomas Gainsborough, (1727-1788), English painter, considered one of the great masters of portraiture and landscape painting. Gainsborough was born in Sudbury, Suffolk. He showed artistic ability at an early age, and when he was 15 years old he studied drawing and etching in London with French engraver Hubert Gravelot. Later he studied painting with Francis Hayman, a painter of historical events. Through Gravelot, who had been a pupil of the great French painter Jean-Antoine Watteau, Gainsborough came under Watteau's influence. Later he was also influenced by the painters of the Dutch school and by Flemish painter Sir Anthony van Dyck. From 1745 to 1760 Gainsborough lived and worked in Ipswich. From 1760 to 1774 he lived in Bath, a fashionable health resort, where he painted numerous portraits and landscapes. In 1768 he was elected one of the original members of the Royal Academy of Arts. In 1774 he painted, by royal invitation, portraits of King George III and the queen consort, Charlotte Sophia. Gainsborough settled in London the same year. He was the favourite painter of the British aristocracy, becoming wealthy through commissions for portraits.

Gainsborough executed more than 500 paintings, of which more than 200 are portraits. His portraits are characterized by the noble and refined grace of the figures, by poetic charm, and by cool and fresh colours, chiefly greens and blues, thinly applied. His most famous portraits include *Orpin, the Parish Clerk* (Tate Gallery, London); *The Baillie Family* (1784) and *Mrs. Siddons* (1785), both in the National Gallery, London; *Perdita Robinson* (1781, Wallace Collection, London); *The Hon. Francis Duncombe* (1777, Frick Collection, New York City); *Mrs. Richard Brinslely Sheridan* (1785-1787, National Gallery of Art, Washington, D.C.); *Mrs. Tenant* (1786-1787, Metropolitan Museum of Art, New York City); and many in private collections, including *The Blue Boy* (1779, Huntington Collection, San Marino, California). His portrait *Mr. and Mrs. Andrews* (1750, National Gallery, London) is unusually balanced between portrait and landscape painting.

The effect of poetic melancholy induced by faint lighting characterizes Gainsborough's paintings. He was obviously influenced by Dutch 17th-century landscape painting. Forest scenes, or rough and broken country, are the usual subjects of his landscapes, most notably *Cornard Wood* (1748) and *The Watering Place* (1777), both in the National Gallery, London. Gainsborough also executed many memorable drawings and etchings.

Famous Work: *Blue Boy.*

❊❊

Francisco José de Goya y Lucientes

Francisco José de Goya y Lucientes, (1746-1828), innovative Spanish painter and etcher; one of the triumvirate—including El Greco and Diego Velázquez—of great Spanish masters. Much in the art of Goya is derived from that of Velázquez, just as much in the art of the 19th-century French master Édouard Manet and the 20th-century genius Pablo Picasso is taken from Goya. Trained in a mediocre rococo artistic milieu, Goya transformed this often frivolous style and created works, such as the famous *Third of May, 1808* (1814, Prado, Madrid), that have as great an impact today as when they were created.

Goya was born in the small Aragonese town of Fuendetodos (near Zaragoza) on March 30, 1746. His father was a painter and a gilder of altarpieces, and his mother was descended from a family of minor Aragonese nobility. Facts of Goya's childhood are scarce. He attended school in Zaragoza at the Escuelas Pias. Goya's formal artistic education commenced when, at the age of 14, he was apprenticed to a local master, José Luzan, a competent although little-known painter in whose studio Goya spent four years. In 1763 the young artist went to Madrid, where he hoped to win a prize at the Academy of San Fernando (founded 1752). Although he did not win the desired award, he did make the acquaintance of Francisco Bayeu, an artist also from Aragón, who was working at the court in the academic manner imported to Spain by the German painter Anton Raphael Mengs. Bayeu (the brother of Goya's wife) was influential in forming Goya's early style and was responsible for his participation in an important commission, the fresco decoration (1771, 1780-1782) of the Church of the Virgin in El Pilar in Zaragoza.

In 1771 Goya went to Italy for approximately one year. His activity there is relatively obscure; he spent some months in Rome and also entered a composition at the Parma Academy competition, in which he was successful. Returning to Spain about 1773, Goya participated in several other fresco projects, including that for the Charterhouse of Aula Dei, near Zaragoza, in 1774, where his paintings prefigure those of his greatest fresco project, executed in the Church of San Antonio de la Florida, Madrid, in 1798. It was at this time that Goya began to do prints after paintings by Velázquez, who would remain, along with Rembrandt, his greatest source of inspiration.

By 1786 Goya was working in an official capacity for King Charles III, the most enlightened Spanish monarch of the 18th century. Goya was appointed first court painter in 1799. His tapestry cartoons executed in the late 1780s and early 1790s were highly praised for their candid views of everyday Spanish life. With these cartoons Goya revolutionized the tapestry industry, which, until that time, had slavishly reproduced the Flemish genre scenes of the 17th-century painter David Teniers. Some of Goya's most beautiful portraits of his friends, members of the court, and the nobility date from the 1780s. Works such as *Marquesa de Pontejos* (1786, National Gallery, Washington, D.C.) show that Goya was then painting in an elegant manner somewhat reminiscent of the style of his English contemporary Thomas Gainsborough.

In the winter of 1792, while on a visit to southern Spain, Goya contracted a serious disease that left him totally deaf and marked a turning point in his career. A mood of pessimism entered Goya's work. Between 1797 and 1799 he drew and etched the first of his great print series *Los caprichos* (The Caprices), which, in their satirical humour, mock the social mores and superstitions of the time. Later series, such as *Desastres de la guerra* (Disasters of War, 1810) and *Disparates* (Absurdities, 1820-1823), present more caustic commentaries on the ills and follies of humanity. The horrors of warfare were of great concern to Goya, who observed firsthand the battles between French soldiers and Spanish citizens during the bloody years of the Napoleonic occupation of Spain. In 1814 he completed *Second of May, 1808* and *Third of May, 1808* (both Prado). These paintings depict horrifying and dramatically brutal massacres of groups of unarmed Spanish street fighters by French soldiers. Both are painted, like so many later pictures by Goya, in thick, bold strokes of dark colour punctuated by brilliant yellow and red highlights.

Straightforward candor and honesty are also present in Goya's later portraits, such as *Family of Charles IV* (1800, Prado), in which the royal family is shown in a completely unidealized fashion, verging on caricature, as a group of strikingly homely individuals.

The *Black Paintings,* scenes of witchcraft and other bizarre activities, are among the most outstanding works of the artist's late years. Executed about 1820, these paintings are now in the Prado. Originally painted in fresco on the walls of Goya's country house and now transferred to canvas, they attest to his progressively darkening mood, possibly aggravated by an oppressive political situation in Spain that forced him to leave for France in 1824. In Bordeaux he took up the then new art of lithography, producing a series of bullfight scenes, considered among the finest lithographs ever made. Although he returned to Madrid for a brief visit in 1826, he died in self-imposed exile in Bordeaux two years later, on April 16, 1828. Goya left no immediate followers of consequence, but his influence was strongly felt in mid-19th-century painting and printmaking and in 20th-century art.

Famous Work: *Maja Nude / Clothed.*

❋❋

Joseph Mallord William Turner

Joseph Mallord William Turner, (1775-1851), English landscape painter, renowned for his vibrant and dramatic treatment of natural light and atmospheric effects in land and marine subjects, and whose work had a direct influence on the development of impressionism. Turner was born in London and studied at the Royal Academy of Arts. At the age of 15 he exhibited his first watercolour at the academy. He would continue to show his work there until 1850. He was elected an associate of the academy in 1799 and a full member three years later. He travelled widely throughout his career, extensively touring England and Scotland and later France, Switzerland, and Italy. In 1807 he became professor of perspective at the Royal Academy and in 1845 he was appointed deputy president.

Turner's early paintings were predominantly watercolours of landscapes. By the late 1790s he had begun exhibiting oil paintings, eventually transferring to his oils the same vibrancy of colour that had proved so successful in his watercolours. His mature work falls into three periods.

Turner's first period (1800-1820) is marked by mythological and historical scenes in which the colouring is subdued and details and contours are emphasized. These works show the influence of 17th-century French landscape painter Claude Lorrain, notably in the use of atmospheric effects, as in *The Sun Rising Through*

Vapor (1807, National Gallery, London), and in the treatment of architectural forms, as in *Dido Building Carthage* (1815, National Gallery). During this period Turner also produced numerous engravings for his unfinished collection *Liber Studiorum* (1806-1819).

The paintings of his second period (1820-1835) are characterized by more brilliant colouring and by diffusion of light. In two of Turner's best works, *The Bay of Baiae—with Apollo and the Sibyl* (1823, Tate Gallery, London) and *Ulysses Deriding Polyphemus* (1829, National Gallery), his use of light lends radiance to the colours and softens architectural and topographical forms and shadows. During this period Turner also executed a number of illustrations for books on topography and a collection of watercolours depicting Venetian scenes.

Turner's artistic genius peaked during his third period (1835-1845). In such works as *Snow Storm: Steam Boat off a Harbour's Mouth* (1842, Tate Gallery), *Peace—Burial at Sea* (1842, Tate Gallery), and *Rain, Steam, and Speed* (1844, National Gallery), he achieved vibrant representations of forces such as the strength of the sea and the rhythm of rain by rendering objects as indistinct masses within a glowing haze of colour. Other famous works of this period include *The Fighting Téméraire* (1839, National Gallery), *The Sun of Venice Going to Sea* (1843, Tate Gallery), and *The Approach to Venice* (1843, National Gallery of Art, Washington, D.C.).

Famous Work: *Rain, Steam, and Speed.*

❊❊

John Constable

John Constable, (1776-1837), English painter, who was a master of landscape painting in the romantic style. His direct studies of nature prompted French painters of the Barbizon School to paint outdoors rather than in the studio. Constable's interest in the effects of light later became an inspiration to the painters of the impressionist movement.

Constable was born in East Bergholt, Suffolk. He showed a strong interest in art from his childhood. After working in his father's flour mill, he went to London in 1799 to study painting at the Royal Academy schools. On his own, Constable also learned painting technique by copying the works of Dutch painter Jacob van Ruisdael and French landscapist Claude Lorrain, both of whom he greatly admired. He exhibited his first landscape paintings in 1802 and thereafter studied painting and English rural life on his own, developing a distinctly individual style.

Constable departed from the traditions of Dutch and English painting by discarding the usual brown underpainting and achieving a more natural and luminous effect through the use of broken bits of colour applied with a palette knife. He was fascinated by reflections in water and light on clouds, and produced many cloud studies. Many of his paintings depict the countryside of the

Stour River valley in Suffolk where he had grown up, and he also portrayed Salisbury and Dorset, in southwest England. He often painted in the open air, but he usually finished his canvases in the studio.

During his lifetime and for many years after his death, Constable received little recognition or support in England. In France, however, where his painting *Hay Wain* (1821, National Gallery, London) was shown by a French dealer at the Paris Salon of 1824, he was much admired by the romantic painter Eugène Delacroix; by the Barbizon painters, who, following Constable's example, began to paint outdoors; and by the impressionists, who sought to capture the effects of light.

Constable's works include *Boatbuilding Near Flatford Mill* (1814-1815, Victoria and Albert Museum, London), which he painted entirely outdoors, *The White Horse* (1819, Frick Collection, New York City), *The Cornfield* (1826, National Gallery, London), and *Salisbury Cathedral from the Meadows* (1831, National Gallery, London). Many small oil sketches are in the Victoria and Albert Museum in London, where they did much to increase his reputation in England. Five of Constable's seven children were painters, and some works formerly attributed to Constable are now known to be the work of his son Lionel.

Famous Work: *The Hay wain.*

❋❋

Dante Gabriel Rossetti

Dante Gabriel Rossetti, (1828-1882), English poet and painter who was a leading member of the Pre-Raphaelite Brotherhood devoted to reviving English art through medieval inspiration. He was born Gabriel Charles Dante Rossetti in London, son of the Italian-born poet Gabriele Rossetti and brother of the poet Christina Rossetti. He was educated at King's College and the Royal Academy in London. At the academy he met the painters Sir John Everett Millais and Holman Hunt, with whom he founded the Pre-Raphaelite Brotherhood. Rossetti was strongly attracted to the dramatic and the supernatural, both of which are represented in his work. Among his earliest paintings was a scene of the annunciation, *Ecce Ancilla Domini* (*The Annunciation,* 1850, Tate Gallery, London). His art subsequently developed through other phases, in which the sense of human beauty, intensity of abstract expression, and richness of colour were leading elements.

Rossetti began writing poetry about the same time that he seriously took to the study of painting. Two of his best-known poems, *The Portrait* and *The Blessed Damozel,* were written in 1842. He made a number of translations from Dante Alighieri and other Italian writers, which were published in 1861 as *The Early Italian Poets.*

Rossetti's later years were marred by sorrow and depression, relieved only by his creative outlets. In 1860 he had married a milliner, Elizabeth Eleanor Siddal, whose beauty he immortalized in many of his best-known paintings, such as *Mary Magdalene at the House of Simon the Pharisee* (1858, Fitzwilliam Museum, Cambridge). Within two years Elizabeth died, and Rossetti was grief stricken by the tragedy. In addition, he was troubled by a bitter attack that had been made on the morality of his poems in an article entitled "The Fleshy School of Poetry," published in *The Contemporary Review* in October 1871. Rossetti's rebuttal was published as "The Stealthy School of Criticism" in the *Athenaeum* in December 1871.

Rossetti continued to produce paintings and poems until late in his life. In 1881 he published *Ballads and Sonnets,* which contained some of his finest work: "*Rose Mary,*" "*The White Ship,*" "*The King's Tragedy,*" and the sonnet sequence *The House of Life.* Of his later paintings, which are murky and dreamlike, two of the best-known are *Dante's Dream* (1871, Walker Art Gallery, Liverpool) and *Proserpina* (1874, Tate Gallery, London).

Famous Work: *Proserpina.*

❋❋

Sir John Everett Millais

Sir John Everett Millais, (1829-96), English painter and illustrator, and a founding member of the artistic movement known as the Pre-Raphaelite Brotherhood.

In 1838 Millais went to London and at the age of 11 entered the Royal Academy schools. Extremely precocious, he won all the academy prizes. In 1848 Millais joined with two other artists, William Holman Hunt and Dante Gabriel Rossetti, to form the Pre-Raphaelite Brotherhood.

The Brotherhood was founded in opposition to contemporary academic painting, which the group believed was the result of the example set by Raphael and which had dominated the schools and academies since his time. At the next year's academy, the novelist Charles Dickens led a violent attack on Millais's "*Christ in the House of His Parents*" (1850; Tate Gallery, London), which many considered blasphemous because of its lack of idealization and seeming irreverence in the use of the mundane.

Millais's period of greatest artistic achievement came in the 1850s. "*The Return of the Dove to the Ark*" (1851; Ashmolean Museum, Oxford) was admired by both the English essayist and critic John Ruskin and the French author Théophile Gautier; and "*The Order of Release*" (1853; Tate Gallery), which included a portrait of his future wife Effie Gray (then unhappily married to Ruskin, whose portrait Millais also painted), was praised by Eugène Delacroix in 1855 and earned for its artist his associateship to the Royal Academy in 1853. In 1856 Millais painted one of his greatest public successes, "*The Blind Girl*" (Birmingham Museums and Art Gallery)—a tour de force of Victorian sentiment and technical facility.

In 1863 Millais became full academician, and by this time his style had broadened and his content altered toward a more deliberately popular, less didactic approach. He executed illustrations for George Dalziel's *Parables* (1864) and E. Moxon's edition of Tennyson's poems and contributed to *Once a Week, Good Words* and other periodicals. Millais's later work is undoubtedly of poorer overall quality—a deterioration of which he was fully aware. In 1870 appeared the first of his pure landscapes, "*Chill October*". Many of these landscapes are of Perthshire, where Millais shot and fished in the autumn. Many portraits belong to this late period, including those of William Gladstone, of Alfred, Lord Tennyson, and of Cardinal Newman. Millais was created a baronet in 1885 and was elected president of the Royal Academy in 1896.

Famous Work: *Ophelia.*

❊❊

Sir Edward Coley Burne-Jones

Sir Edward Coley Burne-Jones, professional name of Edward Coley Jones (1833-1898). One of the leading painters and designers of late 19th-century England, whose romantic paintings using medieval imagery were among the last manifestations of the Pre-Raphaelite style. More long-lasting is his influence as a pioneer of the revival of the ideal of the "artist-craftsman," so influential to the development of 20th-century industrial design.

Burne-Jones was educated at Exeter College, Oxford, where he met his future collaborator, the artist-poet William Morris, then a fellow divinity student. His meeting with the artist Dante Gabriel Rossetti in 1856 marked a turning point in his career, and he left Oxford without graduating. Morris and he then settled in London, working under Rossetti's guidance.

Burne-Jones's vivid imagination delighted in the stories of medieval chivalry, as is seen in his "*King Cophetua and the Beggar Maid*" (1884) and "*Merlin and Nimue*" (1858–59). Stylistically, such works owe much to Rossetti's illustrations, but more often his own dreamworld drew inspiration from the melancholy, attenuated figures of the 15th-century Italian painters Filippino Lippi and Sandro Botticelli, suffusing them with a mood of romantic mysticism. His first big success came with an exhibition in 1877, which included oils such as "*Days of Creation*," "*The Beguiling of*

Merlin" (1872–77), and "*The Mirror of Venus*" (1867–77). From that date until his death, he was increasingly considered to be among the great painters of England. In 1894 he received a baronetcy.

After his death, Burne-Jones's influence was felt far less in painting than in the field of decorative design, particularly in that of ecclesiastical stained glass. He executed reliefs in metals, tiles, and gesso, decorations for pianos and organs, and cartoons for tapestries. Among the latter may be noted the "*Adoration of the Magi*" (Exeter College Chapel, Oxford). Besides several illustrations to other books printed by William Morris' prestigious Kelmscott Press, he made 87 designs for the Kelmscott *Chaucer* of 1896, considered to be among the world's finest printed books.

Famous Work: *The Golden Stairs.*

❋❋

(Hilaire Germain) Edgar Degas

(Hilaire Germain) Edgar Degas, (1834-1917), French painter and sculptor, whose innovative composition, skillful drawing, and perceptive analysis of movement made him one of the masters of modern art in the late 19th century.

Degas is usually classed with the impressionists, and he exhibited with them in seven of the eight impressionist exhibitions. However, his training in classical drafting and his dislike of painting directly from nature produced a style that represented a related alternative to impressionism.

Degas was born into a well-to-do banking family on July 19, 1834, in Paris. He studied at the École des Beaux-Arts under a disciple of the famous French classicist Jean-Auguste-Dominique Ingres, where Degas developed the great drawing ability that was to be a salient characteristic of his art. After 1865, under the influence of the budding impressionist movement, he gave up academic subjects to turn to contemporary themes. But, unlike the impressionists, he preferred to work in the studio and was uninterested in the study of natural light that fascinated them. He was attracted by theatrical subjects, and most of his works depict racecourses, theaters, cafés, music halls, or boudoirs. Degas was a keen observer of humanity—particularly of women, with whom his work is preoccupied—and in his portraits as well as in his studies of dancers, milliners, and laundresses, he

cultivated a complete objectivity, attempting to catch his subjects in poses as natural and spontaneous as those recorded in action photographs.

His study of Japanese prints led him to experiment with unusual visual angles and asymmetrical compositions. His subjects often appear cropped at the edges, as in *Ballet Rehearsal* (1876, Glasgow Art Galleries and Museum). In *Woman with Chrysanthemums* (1865, Metropolitan Museum of Art, New York City), the female subject of the picture is pushed into a corner of the canvas by the large central bouquet of flowers.

In the 1880s, when his eyesight began to fail, Degas began increasingly to work in two new media that did not require intense visual acuity: sculpture and pastel. In his sculpture, as in his paintings, he attempted to catch the action of the moment, and his ballet dancers and female nudes are depicted in poses that make no attempt to conceal their subjects' physical exertions. His pastels are usually simple compositions containing only a few figures. He was obliged to depend on vibrant colours and meaningful gestures rather than on precise lines and careful detailing, but, in spite of such limitations, these works are eloquent and expressive and have a simple grandeur unsurpassed by any of his other works.

Degas was not well-known to the public, and his true artistic stature did not become evident until after his death. He died in Paris on September 27, 1917.

Famous Work: *The Rehearsal.*

❊❊

James Abbott McNeill Whistler

James Abbott McNeill Whistler, (1834-1903), American painter and etcher, who assimilated Japanese art styles, made technical innovations, and championed modern art. Many regard him as pre-eminent among etchers.

Whistler was born on July 10, 1834, in Lowell, Massachusetts. He entered the United States Military Academy at West Point in 1851, did not do well in his studies, and left in 1854 to take a job as a draftsman with the U.S. Coast Survey. One year later he left the United States and went to Paris, where he became a pupil of the Swiss classicist painter Charles Gabriel Gleyre. Formal instruction influenced him less, however, than his acquaintance with the French realist painter Gustave Courbet, other leading contemporary artists, and his own study of the great masters and of Japanese styles.

In Paris, Whistler won recognition as an etcher when his first series of etchings, *Twelve Etchings from Nature* (commonly called *The French Set*), appeared in 1858. Soon after he moved to London, where his paintings, hitherto rejected repeatedly by the galleries of Paris, found acceptance. *At the Piano* was shown by the Royal Academy of London in 1860. In 1863 *Symphony in White No. 1: The White Girl* (National Gallery of Art, Washington, D.C.) won great acclaim in Paris. Thereafter exhibitions of his work aroused increasing international interest, as did his flamboyantly eccentric personality.

Three of Whistler's best-known portraits, *Arrangement in Black and Grey No. 1: The Artist's Mother* (Musée d'Orsay, Paris), *Arrangement in Grey and Black No. 1: Thomas Carlyle* (1872-1874, City Art Gallery and Museum, Glasgow), and *Harmony in Grey and Green: Miss Cicely Alexander* (Tate Gallery, London) were painted around 1872. In 1877 he exhibited a number of landscapes done in the Japanese manner; these paintings, which he called nocturnes, outraged conservative art opinion, which did not understand his avoidance of narrative detail, his layers of atmospheric colour, and his belief in art for art's sake. The English art critic John Ruskin wrote a caustically critical article, and Whistler, charging slander, sued Ruskin for damages. He won the case, one of the most celebrated of its kind, but the expense of the trial forced him into bankruptcy. Selling the contents of his studio, Whistler left England, worked intensively from 1879 to 1880 in Venice, then returned to England and resumed his attack on the academic art tradition.

In later years Whistler devoted himself increasingly to etching, drypoint, lithography, and interior decoration. The *Thames* series (1860), the *First Venice* series (1880), and the *Second Venice* series (1881) heightened his standing as an etcher and won him success when they were exhibited in London in 1881 and 1883. *The Peacock Room*, which he painted for a private London residence (begun 1876 and moved in 1919 to the Freer Gallery of Art, Washington, D.C.), is the most noteworthy example of his interior decoration. Toward the end of his life, when he lived in Paris, Whistler came to be regarded as a major artist. He died in London on July 17, 1903.

Famous Work: *Symphony in White.*

❋❋

Paul Cézanne

Paul Cézanne, (1839-1906), French painter, often called the father of modern art, who strove to develop an ideal synthesis of naturalistic representation, personal expression, and abstract pictorial order.

Among the artists of his time, Cézanne perhaps has had the most profound effect on the art of the 20th century. He was the greatest single influence on both the French artist Henri Matisse, who admired his use of colour, and the Spanish artist Pablo Picasso, who developed Cézanne's planar compositional structure into the cubist style. During the greater part of his own lifetime, however, Cézanne was largely ignored, and he worked in isolation. He mistrusted critics, had few friends, and, until 1895, exhibited only occasionally. He was alienated even from his family, who found his behaviour peculiar and failed to appreciate his revolutionary art.

Cézanne was born in the southern French town of Aix-en-Provence, January 19, 1839, the son of a wealthy banker. His boyhood companion was Émile Zola, who later gained fame as a novelist and man of letters. As did Zola, Cézanne developed artistic interests at an early age, much to the dismay of his father. In 1862, after a number of bitter family disputes, the aspiring artist was given a small allowance and sent to study art in Paris, where Zola had already gone. From the start he was drawn to the more radical elements of the Parisian art world. He especially admired the romantic painter Eugène Delacroix and, among the younger masters, Gustave Courbet and the notorious Édouard Manet, who exhibited realist paintings that were shocking in both style and subject matter to most of their contemporaries.

Many of Cézanne's early works were painted in dark tones applied with heavy, fluid pigment, suggesting the moody, romantic expressionism of previous generations. Just as Zola pursued his interest in the realist novel, however, Cézanne also gradually developed a commitment to the representation of contemporary life, painting the world he observed without concern for thematic idealization or stylistic affectation. The most significant influence on the work of his early maturity proved to be Camille Pissarro, an older but as yet unrecognized painter who lived with his large family in a rural area outside Paris. Pissarro not only provided the moral encouragement that the insecure Cézanne required, but he also introduced him to the new impressionist technique for rendering outdoor light. Along with the painters Claude Monet, Auguste Renoir, and a few others, Pissarro had developed a painting style that involved working outdoors (*en plein air*) rapidly and on a reduced scale, employing small touches of pure colour, generally without the use of preparatory sketches or linear outlines. In such a manner Pissarro and the others hoped to capture the most transient natural effects as well as their own passing emotional states as the artists stood before nature. Under Pissarro's tutelage, and within a very short time during 1872-1873, Cézanne shifted from dark tones to bright hues and began to concentrate on scenes of farmland and rural villages.

Although he seemed less technically accomplished than the other impressionists, Cézanne was accepted by the group and exhibited with them in 1874 and 1877. In general the impressionists did not have much commercial success, and Cézanne's works received the harshest critical commentary. He drifted away from many of his Parisian contacts during the late 1870s and '80s and spent much of his time in his native Aix-en-Provence. After 1882, he did not work closely again with Pissarro. In 1886, Cézanne became embittered over what he took to be thinly disguised references to his own failures in one of Zola's novels. As a result he broke off relations with his oldest supporter. In the same year, he inherited his father's wealth and finally, at the age of 47, became financially independent, but socially he remained quite isolated.

This isolation and Cézanne's concentration and singleness of purpose may account for the remarkable development he sustained during the 1880s and '90s. In this period he continued to paint studies from nature in brilliant impressionist colours, but he gradually simplified his application of the paint to the point where he seemed able to define volumetric forms with juxtaposed strokes of pure colour. Critics eventually argued that Cézanne had discovered a means of rendering both nature's light and nature's form with a single application of colour. He seemed to be reintroducing a formal structure that the impressionists had abandoned, without sacrificing the sense of brilliant illumination they had achieved. Cézanne himself spoke of "modulating" with colour rather than "modeling" with dark and light. By this he meant that he would replace an artificial convention of representation (modeling) with a more expressive system (modulating) that was closer still to nature, or, as the artist himself said, "parallel to nature". For Cézanne, the answer to all the technical problems of impressionism lay in a use of colour both more orderly and more expressive than that of his fellow impressionists.

Cézanne's goal was, in his own mind, never fully attained. He left most of his works unfinished and destroyed many others. He complained of his failure at rendering the human figure, and indeed the great figural works of his last years – such as the *Large Bathers* (circa 1899-1906, Museum of Art, Philadelphia) – reveal curious distortions that seem to have been dictated by the rigor of the system of colour modulation he imposed on his own representations. The succeeding generation of painters, however, eventually came to be receptive to nearly all of Cézanne's idiosyncrasies. Cézanne's heirs felt that the naturalistic painting of impressionism had become formularized, and a new and original style, however difficult it might be, was needed to return a sense of sincerity and commitment to modern art.

For many years Cézanne was known only to his old impressionist colleagues and to a few younger radical post-impressionist artists, including the Dutch painter Vincent van Gogh and the French painter Paul Gauguin. In 1895, however, Ambroise Vollard, an ambitious Paris art dealer, arranged a show of Cézanne's works and over the next few years promoted them successfully. By 1904, Cézanne was featured in a major official exhibition, and by the time of his death (in Aix-en-Provence on October 22, 1906) he had attained the status of a legendary figure. During his last years many younger artists travelled to Aix-en-Provence to observe him at work and to receive any words of wisdom he might offer. Both his style and his theory remained mysterious and cryptic; he seemed to some a naive primitive, while to others he was a sophisticated master of technical procedure. The intensity of his colour, coupled with the apparent rigor of his compositional organization, signaled to most that, despite the artist's own frequent despair, he had synthesized the basic expressive and representational elements of painting in a highly original manner.

Famous Work: *Large Bathers.*

❊❊

Claude Oscar Monet

Claude Oscar Monet, (1840-1926), French painter, a leading figure in the late-19th-century movement called impressionism. Monet's paintings captured scenes of middle-class life and the ever-changing qualities of sunlight in nature. His technique of applying bright, unmixed colours in quick, short strokes became a hallmark of impressionism.

The son of a successful tradesman in marine supplies, Monet grew up in Le Havre on the Normandy coast. He showed signs of artistic talent as a teenager, drawing skillful caricatures of local personalities. He admired the work of many of the more adventurous artists of his day, landscapists associated with the Barbizon School, such as Camille Corot, Charles-François Daubigny, Constant Troyon, and Henri Rousseau. The Barbizon painters promoted landscape painting that stood without reference to historic, religious, or mythological stories, a concept that was then new to French art. Monet also admired French realist artists Gustave Courbet and Honoré Daumier. The realists depicted members of the working classes, who until then had been considered unworthy subjects for art. Monet received crucial early guidance from two artists who specialized in painting seascapes out-of-doors, Eugène Boudin, a fellow painter from Le Havre, and Dutch artist Johan Barthold Jongkind, whom Monet met in 1862. The unusual viewpoints (scenes shown from above or below), and

broad areas of bright colour in Japanese woodblock prints also influenced Monet's work.

Monet's formal art training began in 1859 at the Académie Suisse, a studio that provided models for aspiring artists to draw or paint, but gave little direct instruction. Another future leader of the impressionists, Camille Pissarro, was a fellow student there, and the two soon became close friends. After serving briefly in the French military in Algeria, Monet joined a Parisian studio run by Charles Gabriel Gleyre in 1862. Gleyre's studio was essentially student-run. Like the Adadémie Suisse, it encouraged students to draw from models, rather than from plaster casts of ancient Greek and Roman statues, which was the common teaching method of more conservative academies. In Gleyre's studio Monet met several artists who would become fellow impressionists, Auguste Renoir, Alfred Sisley, and Frédéric Bazille. Bazille, who came from a wealthy family, gave Monet regular financial support during the 1860s.

In 1865 Monet had his first works—two ambitious seascapes–accepted by the Salon, a juried art exhibition sponsored annually by the official French Academy of Fine Arts. Thereafter he had a checkered record of acceptance and rejection by the conservative Salon jury, although his works received praise from critics such as French writer Émile Zola and were purchased by discerning and influential buyers.

Monet's canvases from the mid-1860s were massive. The unfinished *Luncheon on the Grass,* a picnic scene begun in 1865, was originally intended to measure roughly 4.5 m by 6 m (15 ft by 20 ft). For two other large paintings from that time, Monet's future wife Camille Doncieux posed in elegant attire: *The Green Dress* (1866, Kunsthalle, Bremen, Germany), which was shown in the Salon of 1866, and *Women in the Garden* (1867, Musée d'Orsay, Paris). After the Salon rejected *Women in the Garden* for its 1867 exhibition, Monet may have reconsidered investing so much effort in a single painting that might not sell, and he began to work on a smaller scale.

In 1869 Monet and Renoir painted a series of landscapes *en plein air* (outdoors) at a fashionable bathing place, La Grenouillère, on the Seine River near Paris. In these small works, Monet's quick daubs of fresh colours aptly capture the movement of the water and gaiety of the scene.

Despite his father's disapproval, in 1870 Monet married Camille, who had already borne him a son. To escape the Franco-Prussian War (1870-1871), during which German troops threatened Paris, the couple went to London, then to Holland. They returned in 1872 and settled in Argenteuil, a sailing center on the Seine River outside Paris. Monet painted numerous vibrant, light-filled views of this fast-growing suburban town; he also produced more intimate family studies.

The painters who became known as impressionists began exhibiting together in 1874. They held eight exhibitions between 1874 and 1886, and although Monet did not participate in all of these, he became the most celebrated member of the group, and remains so today.

In the 1874 exhibition, Monet showed four pastels and five paintings, among them a work entitled *Impression: Sunrise* (1872-1873, Musée Marmottan, Paris). Inspired by this title, French art critic Louis Leroy coined the term *impressionist* in a satirical review of the exhibition. His comments criticized the artists for painting so loosely and neglecting to blend their brushstrokes carefully in order to achieve the polished effect that was then expected. Although *Impression: Sunrise* is an elegantly balanced composition, it demonstrates much of what was radically new about the impressionist manner. Monet's swift strokes capture a momentary effect of light on water in a busy port, while mist and smoke blur the angular forms of sailboats.

Monet's first wife, Camille, died in 1879, and soon afterward Monet set up home with Alice Hoschedé, the wife of one of his most important patrons, and their respective children. The Hoschedé family had recently suffered a disastrous bankruptcy, and financial concerns seem to have directed many of Monet's career strategies in the years that followed.

In 1880 Monet decided, to the great annoyance of his fellow impressionists, to exhibit once again at the official Salon. He also began to sell his work regularly through private dealers. Monet travelled throughout France during the 1880s, tackling new and challenging motifs, such as the rocks off the island of Belle Île, the stormy Atlantic coast, and the more idyllic atmosphere of the Mediterranean seacoast.

In 1877 Monet had painted a series of works that capture the smoke-filled Saint Lazare railway station in Paris at different times of day. In the 1890s Monet returned to this idea of a concentrated series of paintings based on a single motif. In his series of *Haystacks*, begun in 1890, the rather ordinary subject matter allowed Monet to emphasize subtle changes in light and weather conditions. Each painting has such an individual character that the series also seems to chart Monet's shifting feelings in front of nature. In 1891 French art dealer Paul Durand-Ruel showed 15 of the *Haystack* paintings in his Paris gallery.

Monet followed the *Haystacks* with a *Rouen Cathedral* series (1892-1894). With their heavy encrustations of paint that capture flickering light and shadow, the works challenged accepted understandings of impressionism. The cathedral façade virtually dissolves, and an objective rendering no longer seems to be Monet's goal. With this series, critics began to relate Monet's work to the symbolist movement, in which artists used colour to achieve a highly individual and subjective interpretation of a scene.

Gardens were a recurrent theme for Monet in the 1870s, and paintings of his own garden dominate his later work. In 1890 he purchased a house in Giverny that he had been renting for seven years. He began to develop its gardens, introducing an ornamental lily pond and a Japanese-style bridge. These and other features of his idyllic estate were the subject of a steady output of large decorative paintings. He generally began by painting outdoors, but would then return to his studio to work and rework his canvases, which had become even more layered and complex than before.

Despite frequent periods of financial anxiety, Monet never lacked buyers for his work, and by the 1890s his sales were strong, especially in the United States. The culminating honour of Monet's career was the installation in the Orangerie des Tuileries, a museum in central Paris, of monumental paintings of water lilies, on which he had worked for more than a decade preceding his death. In these works reality seems to dematerialize as he expresses the interplay of colour, light, foliage, and reflection in a tangled mass of brushstrokes. With his eyesight beginning to fail in his final years, Monet explored his subject so closely and thoroughly that the whole dissolved into its parts and began to resemble abstract art.

Famous Work: *Waterlilies.*

❋❋

Berthe Morisot

Berthe Morisot, (1841-1895), French painter and printmaker who exhibited regularly with the Impressionists and, despite the protests of friends and family, continued to participate in their struggle for recognition.

The daughter of a high government official (and a granddaughter of the important Rococo painter Jean-Honoré Fragonard), Morisot decided early to be an artist and pursued her goal with seriousness and dedication. From 1862 to 1868 she worked under the guidance of Camille Corot. She first exhibited paintings at the Salon in 1864. Her work was exhibited there regularly through 1874, when she vowed never to show her paintings in the officially sanctioned forum again. In 1868 she met Édouard Manet, who was to exert a tremendous influence over her work. He did several portraits of her (*e.g.*, "Repose," *c.* 1870). Manet had a liberating effect on her work, and she in turn aroused his interest in outdoor painting.

Morisot's work never lost its Manet-like quality—an insistence on design—nor did she become as involved in colour-optical experimentation as her fellow Impressionists. Her paintings frequently included members of her family, particularly her sister, Edma (*e.g.*, "*The Artist's Sister, Mme Pontillon, Seated on the Grass,*" 1873; and "*The Artist's Sister Edma and Their Mother,*" 1870).

Delicate and subtle, exquisite in colour—often with a subdued emerald glow—they won her the admiration of her Impressionist colleagues. Like that of the other Impressionists, her work was ridiculed by many critics. Never commercially successful during her lifetime, she nevertheless outsold Claude Monet, Pierre-Auguste Renoir, and Alfred Sisley. She was a woman of great culture and charm and counted among her close friends Stéphane Mallarmé, Edgar Degas, Charles Baudelaire, Émile Zola, Emmanuel Chabrier, Renoir, and Monet. She married Édouard Manet's younger brother Eugène.

Famous Work: *The Cradle.*

❊❊

Pierre Auguste Renoir

Pierre Auguste Renoir, (1841-1919), French impressionist painter, noted for his radiant, intimate paintings, particularly of the female nude. Recognized by critics as one of the greatest and most independent painters of his period, Renoir is noted for the harmony of his lines, the brilliance of his colour, and the intimate charm of his wide variety of subjects. Unlike other impressionists he was as much interested in painting the single human figure or family group portraits as he was in landscapes; unlike them, too, he did not subordinate composition and plasticity of form to attempts at rendering the effect of light.

Renoir was born in Limoges on February 25, 1841. As a child he worked in a porcelain factory in Paris, painting designs on china; at 17 he copied paintings on fans, lampshades, and blinds. He studied painting formally in 1862-63 at the academy of the Swiss painter Charles Gabriel Gleyre in Paris. Renoir's early work was influenced by two French artists, Claude Monet in his treatment of light and the romantic painter Eugène Delacroix in his treatment of colour.

Renoir first exhibited his paintings in Paris in 1864, but he did not gain recognition until 1874, at the first exhibition of painters of the new impressionist school. One of the most famous of all impressionist works is Renoir's *Le Bal au Moulin de la Galette* (1876, Louvre, Paris), an open-air scene of a café, in which his mastery in figure painting and in representing light is evident. Outstanding examples of his talents as a portraitist are *Madame Charpentier and Her Children* (1878, The Metropolitan Museum of Art, New York City) and *Jeanne Samary* (1879, Louvre).

Renoir fully established his reputation with a solo exhibition held at the Durand-Ruel Gallery in Paris in 1883. In 1887 he completed a series of studies of a group of nude female figures known as the *Bathers* (Philadelphia Museum of Art). These reveal his extraordinary ability to depict the lustrous, pearly colour and texture of skin and to impart lyrical feeling and plasticity to a subject; they are unsurpassed in the history of modern painting in their representation of feminine grace. Many of his later paintings also treat the same theme in an increasingly bold rhythmic style. During the last 20 years of his life Renoir was crippled by arthritis; unable to move his hands freely, he continued to paint, however, by using a brush strapped to his arm. Renoir died at Cagnes-sur-Mer, a village in the south of France, on December 3, 1919.

Other notable paintings by Renoir include *La Loge* (1874, Courtauld Institute Galleries, London); *Woman with Fan* (1875) and *The Swing* (1875), both in the Louvre, Paris; *The Luncheon of the Boating Party* (1881, Phillips Collection, Washington, D.C.); and *Vase of Chrysanthemums* (1895, Musée de Beaux-Arts, Rouen)—one of the many still lifes of flowers and fruit he painted throughout his life.

Famous Work: *Luncheon of the Boating Party.*

❄❄

Mary Cassatt

Mary Cassatt, (1844-1926), American painter and printmaker who exhibited with the Impressionists.

Cassatt lived in Europe for five years as a young girl. She was tutored privately in art in Philadelphia and attended the Pennsylvania Academy of the Fine Arts in 1861–65, but she preferred learning on her own and in 1866 travelled to Europe to study. Her first major showing was at the Paris Salon of 1872; four more annual Salon exhibitions followed.

In 1874 Cassatt chose Paris as her permanent residence and established her studio there. She shared with the Impressionists an interest in experiment and in using bright colours inspired by the out-of-doors. Edgar Degas became her friend; his style and that of Gustave Courbet inspired her own. Degas was known to admire her drawing especially, and at his request she exhibited with the Impressionists in 1879 and joined them in shows in 1880, 1881, and 1886. Like Degas, Cassatt showed great mastery of drawing, and both artists preferred unposed asymmetrical compositions. Cassatt also was innovative and inventive in exploiting the medium of pastels.

Initially, Cassatt was a figure painter whose subjects were groups of women drinking tea or on outings with friends. After the great exhibition of Japanese prints held in Paris in 1890, she brought out her series of 10 coloured prints—e.g., *Woman Bathing* and *The Coiffure*—in which the influence of the Japanese masters Utamaro and Toyokuni is apparent. In these etchings, combining aquatint, dry point, and soft ground, she brought her printmaking technique to perfection. Her emphasis shifted from form to line and pattern. Soon after 1900 her eyesight began to fail, and by 1914 she had ceased working. The principal motif of her mature and perhaps most familiar period is mothers caring for small children—e.g., *The Bath* (*La Toilette*, c. 1892; Art Institute of Chicago).

Cassatt urged her wealthy American friends and relatives to buy Impressionist paintings, and in this way, more than through her own works, she exerted a lasting influence on American taste. She was largely responsible for selecting the works that make up the H.O. Havemeyer Collection in the Metropolitan Museum of Art, New York City.

Famous Work: *The Bath.*

❋❋

Paul Gauguin

Paul Gauguin, (1848-1903), French post-impressionist painter, whose lush colour, flat two-dimensional forms, and subject matter helped form the basis of modern art.

Eugène Henri Paul Gauguin was born in Paris into a liberal middle-class family. After an adventurous early life, including a four-year stay in Peru with his family and a stint in the French merchant marine, he became a successful Parisian stockbroker, settling into a comfortable bourgeois existence with his wife and five children. In 1874, after meeting the artist Camille Pissarro and viewing the first impressionist exhibition, he became a collector and amateur painter. He exhibited with the impressionists in 1876, 1880, 1881, 1882, and 1886. In 1883 he gave up his secure existence to devote himself to painting; his wife and children, without adequate subsistence, were forced to return to her family. From 1886 to 1891 Gauguin lived mainly in rural Brittany (except for a trip to Panama and Martinique from 1887 to 1888), where he was the center of a small group of experimental painters known as the school of Pont-Aven. Under the influence of the painter Émile Bernard, Gauguin turned away from impressionism and adapted a less naturalistic style, which he called synthetism. He found his inspiration in the art of indigenous peoples, in medieval stained glass, and in Japanese prints; he was introduced to Japanese prints by the Dutch artist Vincent van Gogh when they spent two months together in Arles, in the south of France, in 1888. Gauguin's new style was characterized by the use of large

flat areas of non-naturalistic colour, as in *Yellow Christ* (1889, Albright-Knox Gallery, Buffalo, New York).

In 1891, ruined and in debt, Gauguin sailed for the South Seas to escape European civilization and "everything that is artificial and conventional". Except for one visit to France from 1893 to 1895, he remained in the Tropics for the rest of his life, first in Tahiti and later in the Marquesas Islands. The essential characteristics of his style changed little in the South Seas; he retained the qualities of expressive colour, denial of perspective, and thick, flat forms. Under the influence of the tropical setting and Polynesian culture, however, Gauguin's paintings became more powerful, while the subject matter became more distinctive, the scale larger, and the compositions more simplified. His subjects ranged from scenes of ordinary life, such as *Tahitian Women,* or *On the Beach* (1891, Musée d'Orsay, Paris), to brooding scenes of superstitious dread, such as *Spirit of the Dead Watching* (1892, Albright-Knox Art Gallery). His masterpiece was the monumental allegory *Where Do We Come From? What Are We? Where Are We Going?* (1897, Museum of Fine Arts, Boston), which he painted shortly before his failed suicide attempt. A modest stipend from a Parisian art dealer sustained him until his death at Atuona in the Marquesas on May 9, 1903.

Gauguin's bold experiments in colouring led directly to the 20th-century fauvist style in modern art. His strong modeling influenced the Norwegian artist Edvard Munch and the later expressionist school.

Famous Work: *Nevermore.*

❊❊

Vincent Willem van Gogh

Vincent Willem van Gogh, (1853-1890), Dutch post-impressionist painter, whose work represents the archetype of *expressionism,* the idea of emotional spontaneity in painting. Van Gogh was born March 30, 1853, in Groot-Zundert, son of a Dutch Protestant pastor. Early in life he displayed a moody, restless temperament that was to thwart his every pursuit. By the age of 27 he had been in turn a salesman in an art gallery, a French tutor, a theological student, and an evangelist among the miners at Wasmes in Belgium. His experiences as a preacher are reflected in his first paintings of peasants and potato diggers; of these early works, the best known is the rough, earthy *Potato Eaters* (1885, Rijksmuseum Vincent van Gogh, Amsterdam). Dark and somber, sometimes crude, these early works evidence van Gogh's intense desire to express the misery and poverty of humanity as he saw it among the miners in Belgium.

In 1886 van Gogh went to Paris to live with his brother Théo van Gogh, an art dealer, and became familiar with the new art movements developing at the time. Influenced by the work of the impressionists and by the work of such Japanese printmakers as Hiroshige and Hokusai, van Gogh began to experiment with current techniques. Subsequently, he adopted the brilliant hues found in the paintings of the French artists Camille Pissarro and Georges Seurat.

In 1888 van Gogh left Paris for southern France, where, under the burning sun of Provence, he painted scenes of the fields, cypress trees, peasants, and rustic life characteristic of the region. During this period, living at Arles, he began to use the swirling brush strokes and intense yellows, greens, and blues associated with such typical works as *Bedroom at Arles* (1888, Rijksmuseum Vincent van Gogh), and *Starry Night* (1889, Museum of Modern Art, New York City). For van Gogh all visible phenomena, whether he painted or drew them, seemed to be endowed with a physical and spiritual vitality. In his enthusiasm he induced the painter Paul Gauguin, whom he had met earlier in Paris, to join him. After less than two months they began to have violent disagreements, culminating in a quarrel in which van Gogh wildly threatened Gauguin with a razor; the same night, in deep remorse, van Gogh cut off part of his own ear. For a time he was in a hospital at Arles. He then spent a year in the nearby asylum of Saint-Rémy, working between repeated spells of madness. Under the care of a sympathetic doctor, whose portrait he painted (*Dr. Gachet,*1890, Louvre, Paris), van Gogh spent three months at Auvers. Just after completing his ominous *Crows in the Wheatfields* (1890, Rijksmuseum Vincent van Gogh), he shot himself on July 27, 1890, and died two days later.

The more than 700 letters that van Gogh wrote to his brother Théo (published 1911, translated 1958) constitute a remarkably illuminating record of the life of an artist and a thorough documentation of his unusually fertile output—about 750 paintings and 1600 drawings. The French painter Chaïm Soutine, and the German painters Oskar Kokoschka, Ernst Ludwig Kirchner, and Emil Nolde, owe more to van Gogh than to any other single source. In 1973 the Rijksmuseum Vincent van Gogh, containing over 1000 paintings, sketches, and letters, was opened in Amsterdam.

Famous Work: *Sunflowers.*

❋❋

Georges Seurat

Georges Seurat, (1859-1891), Painter, founder of the 19th-century French school of Neo-Impressionism whose technique for portraying the play of light using tiny brushstrokes of contrasting colours became known as Pointillism. Using this techique, he created huge compositions with tiny, detached strokes of pure colour too small to be distinguished when looking at the entire work but making his paintings shimmer with brilliance. Works in this style include "*Une Baignade, Asnières*" (1883–84) and "*Sunday Afternoon on the Island of La Grande Jatte*" (1884–86).

Georges was the son of Antoine-Chrisostôme Seurat, a 44-year-old property owner, originally from Champagne, and Ernestine Faivre, a Parisienne. His father, a singular personality who had been a bailiff, spent most of his time in Le Raincy, where he owned a cottage with a garden (in which Seurat often painted). The young Seurat lived primarily in Paris with his mother, his brother Émile, and his sister Marie-Berthe. At the time of the Paris Commune, in 1871, when Paris rebelled against the French state and set up its own government, the prudent family temporarily withdrew to Fontainebleau.

While attending school, Georges began to draw, and, beginning in 1875, he took a course from a sculptor, Justin Lequien. He officially entered the École des Beaux-Arts in 1878, in the class of Henri Lehmann, a disciple of Ingres, who painted portraits and conventional nudes. In the school library Seurat discovered a book that was to inspire him for the rest of his life: the *Essai sur les signes inconditionnels de l'art* (1827; "Essay on the Unmistakable Signs of Art"), by Humbert de Superville, a painter-engraver from Geneva; it dealt with the future course of aesthetics and with the relationship between lines and images. Seurat was also impressed with the work of another Genevan aesthetician, David Sutter, who combined mathematics and musicology. Throughout his brief career, Seurat manifested an unusually strong interest in the intellectual and scientific bases of art.

In November 1879, at the age of 20, Seurat went to Brest to do his military service. There he drew the sea, beaches, and boats. When he returned to Paris the following autumn, he shared a studio with another painter, Édmond-François Aman-Jean, who then joined him in Lehmann's class. But Seurat and Aman-Jean departed from the policies of the École des Beaux-Arts in admiring the warm landscapes of Jean-Baptiste Millet at the Louvre. The two friends often frequented dance halls and cabarets in the evening, and in spring they took the passenger steamer to the island of La Grande Jatte, the setting of Seurat's future paintings. Seurat exhibited at the official Salon—the state-sponsored annual exhibition—for the first time in 1883. He displayed portraits of his mother and of his friend Aman-Jean, and in that same year he began his studies, sketches, and panels for "*Une Baignade, Asnières*". When the picture was refused by the jury of the Salon in 1884, Seurat decided to participate in the foundation of the Groupe des Artistes Indépendants, an association "with neither jury nor prizes", where he showed his "*Baignade*" in June.

During this period, he had seen and been strongly influenced by the monumental symbolic paintings of Puvis de Chavannes. He also met the 100-year-old chemist Michel-Eugène Chevreul and experimented with Chevreul's theories of the chromatic circle of light and studied the effects that could be achieved with the three primary colours, yellow, red, and blue, and their complements. Seurat fell in with Paul Signac, who was to become his chief disciple, and painted many rough sketches on small boards in preparation for his masterpiece, "*Sunday Afternoon on the Island of La Grande*

Jatte". In December 1884 he exhibited the "Baignade" again, with the Société des Artistes Indépendents, which was to be of immense influence in the development of modern art.

Seurat spent the winter of 1885 working on the island of La Grande Jatte and the summer at Grandcamp, in Normandy. The Impressionist master Camille Pissarro, who was temporarily converted to the technique of Pointillism, was introduced to Seurat by Signac during this period. Seurat finished the painting "La Grande Jatte" and exhibited it from May 15 to June 15, 1886, at an Impressionist group show. This picture demonstration of his technique aroused great interest. Seurat's chief artistic associates at this time, painters also concerned with the effects of light on colour, were Signac and Pissarro. The unexpectedness of his art and the novelty of his conception excited the Belgian poet Émile Verhaeren. The critic Félix Fénéon praised Seurat's method in an avant-garde review. And Seurat's work was exhibited by the eminent dealer Durand-Ruel in Paris and in New York City.

In 1887, while he was temporarily living in a garret studio, Seurat began work on "*Les Poseuses.*" This painting was to be the last of his compositions on the grand scale of the "Baignade" and "*La Grande Jatte*"; he thought about adding a "*Place Clichy*" to this number but abandoned the idea. In the following year he completed "*Les Poseuses*" and also "*La Parade.*" In February 1888 he went to Brussels with Signac for a private viewing of the exposition of the Twenty (XX), a small group of independent artists, in which he showed seven canvases, including "*La Grande Jatte.*"

Seurat participated in the 1889 Salon des Indépendants, exhibiting landscapes. He painted Signac's portrait at this time. His residence at this point was in the Pigalle district, where he lived with his mistress, Madeleine Knobloch, a girl of 21. On Feb. 16, 1890, Madeleine presented him with a son, whom he officially acknowledged and entered in the register of births under the name of Pierre-Georges Seurat. During that year Seurat completed the painting "*Le Chahut,*" which he sent to the exhibition of the Twenty (XX) in Brussels. During that period he also painted the "*Jeune Femme se poudrant,*" a portrait of his mistress, though he continued to conceal his liaison with her even from his most intimate friends. He spent that summer at Gravelines, near Dunkirk, where he painted several landscapes and planned what was to be his last painting, "*Le Cirque*."

As if from some sort of premonition of his impending death, Seurat showed the uncompleted "Cirque" at the eighth Salon des Indépendants. As an organizer of the exhibition, he exhausted himself in the presentation and hanging of the works. He caught a chill, developed infectious angina, and, before the exhibition was ended, he died on Easter Sunday 1891. On the following day Madeleine Knobloch presented herself at the town hall of her district to identify herself as the mother of Pierre-Georges Seurat. The child, who had contracted his father's contagious illness, died April 13, 1891. Seurat was buried in the family vault at Père Lachaise cemetery. In addition to his seven monumental paintings, he left 40 smaller paintings and sketches, about 500 drawings, and several sketchbooks. Though a modest output in terms of quantity, they show him to have been among the foremost painters of one of the greatest periods in the history of art.

Famous Work: *Sunday Afternoon on the Island of La Grand Jatte.*

❋❋

Henri de Toulouse-Lautrec

Henri de Toulouse-Lautrec, (1864-1901), French post-impressionist painter, lithographer, and illustrator, who documented the bohemian nightlife of late-19th-century Paris.

Toulouse-Lautrec was born in Albi into one of the oldest aristocratic families. He broke both legs as an adolescent, and because of a congenital calcium deficiency, they remained stunted for the rest of his life. During his convalescence, his mother encouraged him to paint. He subsequently studied with French academic painters L. J. F. Bonnat and Fernand Cormon.

Toulouse-Lautrec frequented the Moulin Rouge and other cabarets of the Montmartre district of Paris, where his wit attracted a large group of artists and intellectuals, including Irish author Oscar Wilde, Dutch painter Vincent van Gogh, and French performer Yvette Guilbert. He also frequented the theater, the circus, and Parisian brothels. Toulouse-Lautrec preserved his impressions of these places and their celebrities in portraits and sketches of striking originality and power. Outstanding examples are *La Goulou Entering the Moulin Rouge* (1892, Musée Toulouse-Lautrec, Albi), *Jane Avril Entering the Moulin Rouge* (1892, Courtauld Gallery, London), and *Au salon de la rue des Moulins* (1894, Musée Toulouse-Lautrec). His alcoholic dissipation, however, eventually brought on a paralytic stroke, to which he succumbed at Malromé, one of his family's estates.

Toulouse-Lautrec, many of whose works are in the museum that bears his name in Albi, was a prolific creator. His oeuvre includes great number of paintings, drawings, etchings, lithographs, and posters, as well as illustrations for various contemporary newspapers. He incorporated into his own highly individual method elements of the styles of various contemporary artists, especially French painters Edgar Degas and Paul Gauguin. Japanese art, then coming into vogue in Paris, influenced his use of sharp delineation, asymmetric composition, oblique angles, and flat areas of colour. His work inspired van Gogh, Georges Seurat, and Georges Rouault.

Famous Work: *Aristide Bruant (poster).*

❋❋

Henri Émile Benoît Matisse

Henri Émile Benoît Matisse, (1869-1954), French artist, leader of the fauve group, regarded as one of the great formative figures in 20th-century art, a master of the use of colour and form to convey emotional expression.

Matisse was born in Le Cateau in northern France on December 31, 1869. The son of a middle-class family, he studied and began to practice law. In 1890, however, while recovering slowly from an attack of appendicitis, he became intrigued by the practice of painting. In 1892, having given up his law career, he went to Paris to study art formally. His first teachers were academically trained and relatively conservative; Matisse's own early style was a conventional form of naturalism, and he made many copies after the old masters. He also studied more contemporary art, especially that of the impressionists, and he began to experiment, earning a reputation as a rebellious member of his studio classes.

Matisse's true artistic liberation, in terms of the use of colour to render forms and organize spatial planes, came about first through the influence of the French painters Paul Gauguin and Paul Cézanne and the Dutch artist Vincent van Gogh, whose work he studied closely beginning about 1899. Then, in 1903 and 1904, Matisse encountered the pointillist painting of Henri Edmond Cross and Paul Signac. Cross and Signac were experimenting with juxtaposing small strokes (often dots or "points") of pure pigment to create the strongest visual vibration of intense colour. Matisse adopted their technique and modified it repeatedly, using broader strokes. By 1905 he had produced some of the boldest colour images ever created, including a striking picture of his wife, *Green Stripe* (*Madame Matisse*) (1905, Statens Museum for Kunst, Copenhagen). The title refers to a broad stroke of brilliant green that defines Madame Matisse's brow and nose. In the same year Matisse exhibited this and similar paintings along with works by his artist companions, including André Derain and Maurice de Vlaminck. Together, the group was dubbed *les fauves* (literally, "the wild beasts") because of the extremes of emotionalism in which they seemed to have indulged, their use of vivid colours, and their distortion of shapes.

While he was regarded as a leader of radicalism in the arts, Matisse was beginning to gain the approval of a number of influential critics and collectors, including the American expatriate writer Gertrude Stein and her family. Among the many important commissions he received was that of a Russian collector who requested mural panels illustrating dance and music (both completed in 1911; now in the Hermitage, Saint Petersburg). Such broadly conceived themes ideally suited Matisse; they allowed him freedom of invention and play of form and expression. His images of dancers, and of human figures in general, convey expressive form first and the particular details of anatomy only secondarily. Matisse extended this principle into other fields; his bronze sculptures, like his drawings and works in several graphic media, reveal the same expressive contours seen in his paintings.

Although intellectually sophisticated, Matisse always emphasized the importance of instinct and intuition in the production of a work of art. He argued that an artist did not have complete control over colour and form; instead, colours, shapes, and lines would come to dictate to the sensitive artist how they might be employed in relation to one another. He often emphasized his joy in abandoning himself to the play of the forces of colour and design, and he explained the rhythmic, but distorted, forms of many of his figures in terms of the working out of a total pictorial harmony.

From the 1920s until his death, Matisse spent much time in the south of France, particularly Nice, painting local scenes with a thin, fluid application of bright colour. In his old age, he was commissioned to design the decoration of the small Chapel of Saint-Marie du Rosaire at Vence (near Cannes), which he completed between 1947 and 1951. Often bedridden during his last years, he occupied himself with decoupage, creating works of brilliantly coloured paper cutouts arranged casually, but with an unfailing eye for design, on a canvas surface.

Matisse died in Nice on November 3, 1954. Unlike many artists, he was internationally popular during his lifetime, enjoying the favour of collectors, art critics, and the younger generation of artists.

Famous Work: *The Dance.*

❋❋

Piet Mondrian

Piet Mondrian, (1872-1944), Dutch painter, who carried abstraction to its furthest limits. Through radical simplification of composition and colour, he sought to expose the basic principles that underlie all appearances.

Born in Amersfoort, the Netherlands, on March 7, 1872, and originally named Pieter Cornelis Mondriaan, Mondrian embarked on an artistic career over his family's objections, studying at the Amsterdam Academy of Fine Arts. His early works, through 1907, were calm landscapes painted in delicate grays, mauves, and dark greens. In 1908, under the influence of the Dutch painter Jan Toorop, he began to experiment with brighter colours; this represented the beginning of his attempts to transcend nature. Moving to Paris in 1911, Mondrian adopted a cubist-influenced style, producing analytical series such as *Trees* (1912-1913) and *Scaffoldings* (1912-1914). He moved progressively from semi-naturalism through increased abstraction, arriving finally at a style in which he limited himself to small vertical and horizontal brushstrokes.

In 1917 Mondrian and the Dutch painter Theo van Doesburg founded *De Stijl* magazine, in which Mondrian developed his theories of a new art form he called neoplasticism. He maintained that art should not concern itself with reproducing images of real objects, but should express only the universal absolutes that underlie reality. He rejected all sensuous qualities of texture, surface, and colour, reducing his palette to flat primary colours. His belief that a canvas—a plane surface—should contain only planar elements led to his abolition of all curved lines in favour of straight lines and right angles. His masterly application of these theories led to such works as *Composition with Red, Yellow, and Blue* (1937-1942, Tate Gallery, London), in which the painting, composed solely of a few black lines and well-balanced blocks of colour, creates a monumental effect out of all proportion to its carefully limited means.

When Mondrian moved to New York City in 1940, his style became freer and more rhythmic, and he abandoned severe black lines in favour of lively chain-link patterns of bright colours, particularly notable in his last complete masterwork, *Broadway Boogie Woogie* (1942-1943, Museum of Modern Art, New York City).

Mondrian was one of the most influential 20th-century artists. His theories of abstraction and simplification not only altered the course of painting but also exerted a profound influence on architecture, industrial design, and the graphic arts. Mondrian died in New York on February 1, 1944.

Famous Work: *Broadway Boogie Woogie.*

❊❊

Pablo Ruiz y Picasso

Pablo Ruiz y Picasso, (1881-1973), Spanish painter, who is widely acknowledged to be the most important artist of the 20th century. A long-lived and highly prolific artist, he experimented with a wide range of styles and themes throughout his career. Among Picasso's many contributions to the history of art, his most important include pioneering the modern art movement called cubism, inventing collage as an artistic technique, and developing assemblage (constructions of various materials) in sculpture.

Picasso was born Pablo Ruiz in Málaga, Spain. He later adopted his mother's more distinguished maiden name—Picasso—as his own. Though Spanish by birth, Picasso lived most of his life in France.

Picasso's father, who was an art teacher, quickly recognized that his child Pablo was a prodigy. Picasso studied art first privately with his father and then at the Academy of Fine Arts in La Coruña, Spain, where his father taught. Picasso's early drawings, such as *Study of a Torso, After a Plaster Cast* (1894-1895, Musée Picasso, Paris, France), demonstrate the high level of technical proficiency he had achieved by 14 years of age. In 1895 his family moved to Barcelona, Spain, after his father obtained a teaching post at that city's Academy of Fine Arts. Picasso was admitted to advanced classes at the academy after he completed in a single day the entrance examination that applicants traditionally were given a month to finish. In 1897 Picasso left Barcelona to study at the Madrid Academy in the Spanish capital. Dissatisfied with the training, he quit and returned to Barcelona.

After Picasso visited Paris in October 1900, he moved back and forth between France and Spain until 1904, when he settled in the French capital. In Paris he encountered, and experimented with, a number of modern artistic styles. Picasso's painting *Le Moulin de la Galette* (1900, Guggenheim Museum, New York City) revealed his interest in the subject matter of Parisian nightlife and in the style of French painter Henri de Toulouse-Lautrec, a style that verged on caricature. In addition to café scenes, Picasso painted landscapes, still lifes, and portraits of friends and performers.

From 1901 to 1903 Picasso initiated his first truly original style, which is known as the blue period. Restricting his colour scheme to blue, Picasso depicted emaciated and forlorn figures whose body language and clothing bespeak the lowliness of their social status. In *The Old Guitarist* (1903, Art Institute of Chicago, Illinois), Picasso emphasized the guitarist's poverty and position as a social outcast, which he reinforced by surrounding the figure with a black outline, as if to cut him off from his environment. The guitarist is compressed within the canvas (no room is left in the painting for the guitarist to raise his lowered head), suggesting his helplessness: The guitarist is trapped within the frame just as he is trapped by his poverty. Although Picasso underscored the squalor of his figures during this period, neither their clothing nor their environment conveys a specific time or place. This lack of specificity suggests that Picasso intended to make a general statement about human alienation rather than a particular statement about the lower class in Paris.

Why blue dominated Picasso's paintings during this period remains unexplained. Possible influences include photographs with a bluish tinge popular at the time, poetry that stressed the colour blue in its imagery, or the paintings of French artists such as Eugène Carrière or Claude Monet, who based many of their works around this time on variations on a single colour. Another explanation is that Picasso found blue particularly appropriate for his subject matter because it is a colour associated with melancholy.

In 1904 Picasso's style shifted, inaugurating the rose period, sometimes referred to as the circus period. Although Picasso still focused on social outcasts—especially circus performers—his colour scheme lightened, featuring warmer, reddish hues, and the thick outlines of the blue period disappeared. Picasso maintained his interest in the theme of alienation, however. In *Two Acrobats and a Dog* (1905, Museum of Modern Art, New York City), he represented two young acrobats before an undefined, barren landscape. Although the acrobats are physically close, they gaze in different directions and do not interact, and the reason for their presence is not made clear. Differences in the acrobats' height also exaggerate their disconnection from each other and from the empty landscape. The dog was a frequent presence in Picasso's work and may have been a reference to death as dogs appear at the feet of figures in many Spanish funerary monuments.

Picasso may have felt an especially deep sympathy for circus performers. Like artists, they were paid to entertain society, but their itinerant lifestyle and status as outsiders prevented them from becoming an integral part of the social fabric. It was this situation that made the sad clown an important figure in the popular imagination: Paid to make people laugh, he must keep hidden his real existence and true feelings. Living a life of financial insecurity himself, Picasso no doubt empathized with these performers. During this period Picasso met Fernande Olivier, the first of several women who shared his life and provided inspiration for his art. Olivier's features appear in many of the female figures in his paintings over the next several years.

Experimentation and rapid style changes mark the years from late 1905 on. Picasso's paintings from late 1905 are more emotionally detached than those of the blue or rose periods. The colour scheme lightens—beiges and light browns predominate—and melancholy and alienation give way to a more reasoned approach. Picasso's increasing interest in form is apparent in his references to classical sculpture. The figure of a seated boy in *Two Youths* (1905, National Gallery, Washington, D.C.), for example, recalls an ancient Greek sculpture of a boy removing a thorn from his foot.

By 1906 Picasso had become interested in sculptures from the Iberian peninsula dating from about the 6th to the 3rd century BC. Picasso must have found them of particular interest both because they are native to Spain and because they display remarkable simplification of form. The Iberian influence is immediately visible in *Self-Portrait* (1906, Philadelphia Museum of Art, Pennsylvania), in which Picasso reduced the image of his head to an oval and his eyes to almond shapes, thus revealing his increasing fascination with geometric simplification of form.

Picasso's predilection for experimentation and for drawing inspiration from outside the accepted artistic sources led to his most radical and revolutionary painting yet in 1907: *The Demoiselles d'Avignon* (1907, Museum of Modern Art). The painting's theme—the female nude—could not be more traditional, but Picasso's treatment of it is revolutionary. Picasso took even greater liberties here with human anatomy than in his 1906 *Self-Portrait* . The figures on the left in the painting look flat, as if they have no skeletal or muscular structure. Faces seen from the front have noses in profile. The eyes are asymmetrical and radically simplified. Contour lines are incomplete. Colour juxtapositions—between blue and orange, for instance—are intentionally strident and unharmonious. The representation of space is fragmented and discontinuous.

While the left side of the canvas is largely Iberian-influenced, the right side is inspired by African masks, especially in its striped patterns and oval forms. Such borrowings, which led to great simplification, distortion, and visual incongruities, were considered extremely daring in 1907. The head of the figure at the bottom right, for example, turns in an anatomically impossible way. These discrepancies proved so shocking that even Picasso's fellow painters reacted negatively to *The Demoiselles d'Avignon*. French painter Henri Matisse allegedly told Picasso that he was trying to ridicule the modern movement.

For many scholars, *The Demoiselles d'Avignon*—with its fragmented planes, flattened figures, and borrowings from African masks—marks the beginning of the new visual language, known as cubism. Other scholars believe that French painter Paul Cézanne provided the primary catalyst for this change in style. Cézanne's work of the 1890s and early 1900s was noted both for its simplification and flattening of form and for the introduction of what art historians call *passage,* the interpenetration of one physical object by another. For example, in *Mont Sainte-Victoire* (1902-1906, Metropolitan Museum of Art, New York City), Cézanne left the outer edge of the mountain open, allowing the blue area of the sky and the gray area of the mountain to merge. This innovation—air and rock interpenetrating—was a crucial precedent for Picasso's invention of cubism. First, it defied the laws of our physical experience, and second, it indicated that artists were viewing paintings as having a logic of their own that functioned independently of, or even contrary to, the logic of everyday experience.

Scholars generally divide the cubist innovations of Picasso and French painter Georges Braque into two stages. In the first stage, analytical cubism, the artists fragmented three-dimensional shapes into multiple geometric planes. In the second stage, synthetic cubism, they reversed the process, putting abstract planes together to represent human figures, still lifes, and other recognizable shapes.

Profoundly influenced by Cézanne's later work, Picasso and Braque initiated a series of landscape paintings in 1908. These paintings approximated Cézanne's both in their colour scheme (dark greens and light browns) and in their drastic simplification of nature to geometric shapes. Upon seeing these paintings, French critic Louis Vauxelles coined the term *cubism*. In Picasso's *Houses on the Hill, Horta de Ebro* (1909, Museum of Modern Art), he gave architectural structures a three-dimensional, cubic quality, but he abandoned conventional three-dimensional perspective: Instead of being depicted one behind the other, buildings appear one on top of the other. Moreover, he simplified every aspect of the painting according to a vocabulary of cubic shapes—not just the houses but the sky as well. By neutralizing differences between earth and sky, Picasso made the canvas appear more unified, but he also introduced ambiguity by not differentiating solid from void. In addition, Picasso often used inconsistent light sources. In some parts of a painting, light appears to come from the left; in other parts, it comes from the right, the top, or even the bottom. Spatial planes intersect in ways that leave the spectator guessing whether angles are concave or convex. Delight in confusing the viewer is a regular feature of cubism.

By 1910, it had become evident that cubism no longer had any cubes and that the illusion of three-dimensional space, or volume, was gone. Picasso seemed to have dismantled the very idea of solid form, not only by fragmenting the human figure and other shapes, but also by using Cézanne's concept of passage to merge figure and environment, solid and void, background and foreground. In this way he created a visually consistent painting, yet the consistency does not conform to the physical consistency of the natural world as we experience it. Picasso's decision to limit his colour scheme to dark browns and grays also suggests that his paintings have initiated a radical departure from nature, rather than attempted to copy it.

The year 1912 marks another major development in the cubist language: the invention of collage. In *Still Life with Chair Caning* (1912, Musée Picasso), Picasso attached a piece of oilcloth (that depicts woven caning) to his work. With this action Picasso not only violated the integrity of the medium—oil painting on canvas—but also included a material that had no previous connection with high art. Art could now be created, Picasso seems to imply, with scissors and glue as well as with paint and canvas. By including pieces of cloth, newspaper, wallpaper, advertising, and other materials in his work, Picasso opened the door for any object or material, however ordinary, to be included in (or even replace) a work of art. This innovation had important consequences for later 20th-century art. Another innovation was including the letters JOU in the painting, possibly referring to the beginning of the word *journal* (French for "newspaper") or to the French word *jouer,* meaning "to play," as Picasso is playing with forms. These combinations reveal that cubism includes both visual and verbal references, and merges high art with popular culture.

By inventing collage and by introducing elements from the real world in his canvases, Picasso avoided taking cubism to the level of complete abstraction and remained in the domain of tangible objects. Collage also initiated the synthetic phase of cubism. Whereas analytical cubism fragmented figures into geometric planes, synthetic cubism *synthesized* (combined) near-abstract shapes to create representational forms, such as a human figure or still life. Synthetic cubism also tended toward multiplicity. In *Guitar, Sheet Music, and Wine Glass* (1912, McNay Art Museum, San Antonio, Texas), for instance, Picasso combined a drawing of a glass, several spots of colour, sheet music, newspaper, a wallpaper pattern, and a cloth that has a wood–grain pattern. Synthetic cubism may also combine different textures, such as wood grain, sand, and printed matter. Sometimes Picasso applied these textures as collage, by gluing textured papers on the canvas. In other cases the artist painted an area to look like wood or wallpaper, fooling the spectator by means of visual puns.

In 1912 Picasso instigated another important innovation: construction, or assemblage, in sculpture. Before this innovation, sculpture, at least in the West, was primarily created in one of two ways: by carving a block of stone or wood or by modeling—shaping a form in clay and casting that form in a more durable material, such as bronze. In *Guitar* (1912, Museum of Modern Art), Picasso used a new additive process. He cut various shapes out of sheet metal and wire, and then reassembled those materials into a cubist construction. In other constructions, Picasso used wood, cardboard, string, and other everyday objects, not only inventing a new technique for sculpture but also expanding the definition of art by blurring the distinction between artistic and non-artistic materials.

From World War I (1914-1918) onward, Picasso moved from style to style. In 1915, for instance, Picasso painted the highly abstract *Harlequin* (Museum of Modern Art) and drew the highly realistic portrait of *Ambroise Vollard* (Metropolitan Museum of Art). During and after the war he also worked on stage design and costume design for the Ballets Russes, a modern Russian ballet company launched by the impresario Sergey Diaghilev. Inspired by his direct experience of the theater, Picasso also produced representations of performers, such as French clowns called Pierrot and Harlequin, and scenes of ballerinas.

Picasso separated from Olivier in 1912, after meeting Eva Gouel. Gouel died in 1915, and in 1918 Picasso married Olga Koklova, one of the dancers in Diaghilev's company. Picasso created a number of portraits of her, and their son, Paulo, appears in works such as *Paulo as Harlequin* (1924, Musée Picasso).

After World War I, a strain of conservatism spread through a number of art forms. A motto popular among traditionalists was "the return to order". For Picasso the years 1920 to 1925 were marked by close attention to three-dimensional form and to classical themes: bathers, *centaurs* (mythical creatures half-man and half horse), and women in classical drapery. He depicted many of these figures as massive, dense, and weighty, an effect intensified by strong contrasts of light and dark. But even as he moved toward greater realism, Picasso continued to play games with the viewer. In the classical and carefully composed *The Pipes of Pan* (1923, Musée Picasso), for example, he painted an area of the architectural framework in the foreground (which should be grayish) with the same colour as the sea in the background, revealing again his pleasure in ambiguity.

From 1925 to 1936 Picasso again worked in a number of styles. He composed some paintings of tightly structured geometric shapes, limiting his colour scheme to primary colours (red, blue, yellow), as in *The Studio* (1928, Museum of Modern Art). In other paintings, such as *Nude in an Armchair* (1929, Musée Picasso), he depicted contorted female figures whose open mouths and menacing teeth reveal a more emotional, less reasoned attitude. Picasso's marriage broke up during this time, and some of the menacing female figures in his art of this period may represent Koklova.

The same diversity is visible in Picasso's sculpture during this period. *Bather (Metamorphosis II)* (1928, Musée Picasso) represents the human body as a massive spherical shape with protruding limbs, whereas *Wire Construction* (1928, Musée Picasso) depicts it as a rigid, geometric configuration of thin wires. Picasso also experimented with welding in sculpture of this period and explored a variety of themes, including the female head, the sleeping woman, and the Crucifixion. The model for many of his sleeping women was Marie Thérèse Walter, a new love who had entered his life. Their daughter, Maia, was born in 1935.

In the early 1930s Picasso had increasing contact with the members of the surrealist movement and became fascinated with the classical myth of the Minotaur. This creature, which has the head of a man and the body of a bull, appears in a study by Picasso for the cover of the surrealist journal *Minotaure* (1933, Museum of Modern Art). Here Picasso affixed a classical drawing of a Minotaur to a collage of abstracted forms and debris. The Minotaur has numerous incarnations in Picasso's work, both as an aggressor and a victim, as a violent character and a friendly one. It may represent the artist himself and frequently appears in the context of a bullfight, a typically Spanish scene close to Picasso's heart.

In 1937 the Spanish government commissioned Picasso to create a mural for Spain's pavilion at an international exposition in Paris. Unsure about the subject, Picasso procrastinated. But he set to work almost immediately after hearing that the Spanish town of Guernica had been bombed by Nazi warplanes in support of Spanish general Francisco Franco's plot to overthrow the Spanish republic. *Guernica* (1937, Prado, Madrid) was Picasso's response to, and condemnation of, that event. He executed the painting in black and white—in keeping with the seriousness of the subject–and transfigured the event according to his fascination with the bullfight theme.

At the extreme left is a bull, which symbolizes brutality and darkness, according to Picasso. At the center, a horse wounded by a spear most likely represents the Spanish people. At the center on top, an exploding light bulb possibly refers to air warfare or to evil coming from above (and putting out the light of reason). Corpses and dying figures fill the foreground: a woman with a dead child at the left, a dead warrior with a broken sword (from which a flower sprouts) at the center, a weeping woman and a figure falling through a burning building at the right. The distortion of these figures expresses the inhumanity of the event. To suggest the screaming of the horse and of the mother with the dead child, Picasso transformed their tongues into daggers. In the upper center, a tormented female figure holds an oil lamp that sheds light upon the scene, possibly symbolizing the light of truth revealing the brutality of the event to the outside world. In 1936 Picasso met Dora Maar, an artist who photographed *Guernica* as he painted it. She soon became his companion and the subject of his paintings, although he remained involved with Walter.

Picasso, unlike many artists, stayed in Paris during the German occupation of World War II. Some of his paintings from this time reveal the anxiety of the war years, as does the menacing *Still Life with Steer's Skull* (1942, Kunstsammlung Nordrhein-Westfalen, Düsseldorf, Germany). Other works, such as his sculpture *Head of a Bull* (1943, Musée Picasso), are more playful and whimsical. In this sculpture Picasso combined a bicycle seat and handlebars to represent the bull's head. Upon receiving news of the Nazi death camps, Picasso also painted, although he did not finish, an homage to the victims of the Holocaust (mass murder of European Jews during the war). In this painting, called *The Charnel House* (1945, Museum of Modern Art), he restricted the colour scheme to black and white (as in *Guernica*) and depicted an accumulation of distorted, mangled bodies. During the war Picasso joined the Communist Party, and after the war he attended several peace conferences.

Picasso remained a prolific artist until late in his life, although this later period has not received universal acclaim from historians or critics. He made variations on motifs that had fascinated him throughout his career, such as the bullfight and the painter and his model, the latter a theme that celebrated creativity. And he continued to paint portraits and landscapes. Picasso also experimented with ceramics, creating figurines, plates, and jugs, and he thereby blurred an existing distinction between fine art and craft.

Picasso's emotional life became more complicated after he met French painter Françoise Gilot in the 1940s, while he was still involved with Maar. He and Gilot had a son, Claude, and a daughter, Paloma, and both appear in many of his late works. Picasso and Gilot parted in 1953. Jacqueline Roque, whom Picasso married in 1961, became his next companion. They spent most of their time in the south of France.

Another new direction in Picasso's work came from variations on well-known works by older artists that he recast in his own style. Among these works are *Women on the Banks of the Seine, after Courbet* (1950, Kunstmuseum, Basel, Switzerland) and *Le Déjeuner sur l'Herbe after Manet* (1960, Musée Picasso). What makes these works particularly significant is that they run counter to a basic premise of modern art, Picasso's included: namely, originality. Although many modern painters were influenced by earlier artists, they rarely made such direct and obvious references to each other's work because they deemed such references unoriginal. In the postmodern period, which began in the 1970s, artists and critics began to question the modernist directive to be original. In acts of deliberate defiance, many post-modern artists have *appropriated* (taken for their own use) well-known images from their predecessors or contemporaries. Seen against this context, Picasso's later variations on paintings by earlier masters hardly seem out of place; on the contrary, they anticipate a key aspect of art in the 1980s.

One of Picasso's late works, *Head of a Woman* (1967), was a gift to the city of Chicago. This sculpture of welded steel, 15 m (50 ft) tall, stands in front of Chicago's Civic Center. Although its semi-abstract form proved controversial at first, the sculpture soon became a city landmark.

Because of his many innovations, Picasso is widely considered to be the most influential artist of the 20th century. The cubist movement, which he and Braque inspired, had a number of followers. Its innovations gave rise to a host of other 20th-century art movements, including futurism in Italy, suprematism and constructivism in Russia, de Stijl in the Netherlands, and vorticism in England. Cubism also influenced German expressionism, dada, and other movements as well as early work of the surrealists and abstract expressionists. In addition, collage and construction became key aspects of 20th-century art.

Famous Work: *Guernica.*

❊❊

Salvador Dalí

Salvador Dalí, (1904-1989), Spanish Surrealist painter and printmaker, influential for his explorations of subconscious imagery.

As an art student in Madrid and Barcelona, Dalí assimilated a vast number of artistic styles and displayed unusual technical facility as a painter. It was not until the late 1920s, however, that two events brought about the development of his mature artistic style: his discovery of Sigmund Freud's writings on the erotic significance of subconscious imagery, and his affiliation with the Paris Surrealists, a group of artists and writers who sought to establish the "greater reality" of man's subconscious over his reason. To bring up images from his subconscious mind, Dalí began to induce hallucinatory states in himself by a process he described as "paranoiac critical".

Once Dalí hit on this method, his painting style matured with extraordinary rapidity, and from 1929 to 1937 he produced the paintings which made him the world's best-known Surrealist artist. He depicted a dream world in which commonplace objects are juxtaposed, deformed, or otherwise metamorphosed in a bizarre and irrational fashion. Dalí portrayed these objects in meticulous, almost painfully realistic detail and usually placed them within bleak, sunlit landscapes that were reminiscent of his Catalonian homeland. Perhaps the most famous of these enigmatic images is "*The Persistence of Memory*" (1931), in which limp, melting watches rest in an eerily calm landscape. With the Spanish director Luis Buñuel, Dalí also made two Surrealistic films—*Un Chien andalou* (1928; *An Andalusian Dog*) and *L'Âge d'or* (1930; *The Golden Age*)—that are similarly filled with grotesque but highly suggestive images.

In the late 1930s Dalí switched to painting in a more academic style under the influence of the Renaissance painter Raphael, and as a consequence he was expelled from the Surrealist movement. Thereafter he spent much of his time designing theatre sets, interiors of fashionable shops, and jewellery, as well as exhibiting his genius for flamboyant self-promotional stunts in the United States, where he lived from 1940 to 1955. In the period from 1950 to 1970 Dalí painted many works with religious themes, though he continued to explore erotic subjects, to represent childhood memories, and to use themes centring on his wife, Gala. Notwithstanding their technical accomplishments, these later paintings are not as highly regarded as the artist's earlier works. The most interesting and revealing of Dalí's books is *The Secret Life of Salvador Dali* (1942–44).

Famous Work: *The persistence of Memory.*

❋❋

Francis Bacon

Francis Bacon, (1909-1992), Irish-born British artist noted for paintings in which the human body is bizarrely, even terrifyingly, distorted. Bacon's achievement as one of the most powerful figure painters of the 20th century is all the more remarkable because he emerged as a figure painter in the 1940s and 1950s, an artistic era dominated by abstraction.

The figures in Bacon's paintings are blurred and twisted and are typically confined within mysterious arenas or boxlike enclosures. Critics stress the horror and violence in Bacon's pictures. But Bacon himself felt a kinship with old masters, including Spanish baroque artist Diego Velázquez and Italian Renaissance artist Michelangelo, and with 19th-century photographer Eadweard Muybridge. Muybridge used photographs to study the body in motion, and the blurring in Bacon's paintings suggests blurred photographs of moving bodies. Many of Bacon's paintings refer to specific art works from the past. In 1949 he painted the first of a series of so-called Screaming Popes, which were based on a Velázquez portrait of *Pope Innocent X* (1649-1650, Palazzo Doria-Pamphili, Rome). In Bacon's paintings, the popes' mouths are distorted, and the figures appear as if caged in glass. Later, Bacon concentrated on a series of triptychs (three-paneled paintings) based on a 13th-century depiction of the crucifixion of Christ. An example from this series is *Three Studies for a Crucifixion* (1962, Solomon R. Guggenheim Museum, New York), with mutilated male figures set in nightmarish rooms. Throughout his career, Bacon also painted powerful self-portraits and portraits of his friends.

Bacon was born to English parents in Dublin, Ireland, and brought up in Ireland and England. In 1925 he left home, going to London and then on to Berlin and Paris. In Paris he began to take an interest in painting. An exhibition in Paris of works by Spanish painter Pablo Picasso appears in particular to have inspired him. By 1929 he was back in London, and his earliest works from this period reflect the influence of cubism, a style pioneered by Picasso. Moreover, the distorted, elongated figures that Bacon painted soon afterward seem to draw on Picasso's biomorphic forms of the late 1920s. Bacon was entirely self-taught as a painter, and his work remained for the most part unknown until the late 1940s. In 1954, he was selected to represent Britain at the Venice Biennale, a major international art exhibition. Bacon enjoyed international renown during the 1980s, when figurative painting regained prominence in the United States and Europe.

Famous Work: *Study after Velazquez's Portrait of Pope Innocent X.*

❋❋

Jackson Pollock

Jackson Pollock, (1912-1956), American abstract painter, who developed a technique for applying paint by pouring or dripping it onto canvases laid on the floor. With this method Pollock produced intricate interlaced webs of paint, as in *Black and White* (1948, private collection). Rapid and seemingly impulsive execution like Pollock's became a hallmark of abstract expressionism, a movement that emphasized the spontaneous gestures of the artist.

Born in Cody, Wyoming, Pollock moved to New York City in 1930 to study at the Art Students League with American artist Thomas Hart Benton. Pollock's early paintings, realistic scenes of life in America, clearly reflect Benton's influence. As his career progressed, Pollock rejected his teacher's representational subject matter, but retained Benton's emphasis on rhythmic, dynamic composition. In New York, Pollock was also exposed to the work of Mexican mural painters José Clemente Orozco and David Alfaro Siqueiros. Their experimental techniques, large scale, and use of industrial paints had a lasting impact on Pollock's work.

The surrealism movement was another significant influence upon Pollock, whose ideas about the relevance of the unconscious to artistic creativity coincided with his own experience. As part of treatment for alcoholism, Pollock underwent psychoanalysis; his therapists, who followed the teachings of Swiss psychiatrist Carl Gustav Jung, encouraged him to analyze his drawings for clues to his unconscious mental processes. Surrealist artists had also hoped to tap into the unconscious through *automatism,* a technique in which the artist's hand wanders across the painting's surface with as little conscious control as possible. In early works such as *The She-Wolf* (1943, Museum of Modern Art, New York City), Pollock combined surrealist automatism with subject matter that reflects his interests in ancient sculpture, non-Western art, and the work of Spanish artist Pablo Picasso.

After moving to a larger studio on Long Island in 1947, Pollock began creating his characteristic large-scale abstractions. He placed the canvas on the floor, attacked it from all directions, and poured paint directly on it. His new method resulted in part from his interest in Native American sand paintings, which are created on the ground with sand of various colours let loose from the hand. Typical of this period, *Autumn Rhythm* (1950, Metropolitan Museum of Art, New York City) is clearly abstract, since it makes no direct reference to the external world. However, Pollock described his abstraction as an attempt to evoke the rhythmic energy of nature (as the title *Autumn Rhythm* indicates).

Pollock reinforced this dynamism with compositions that emphasized all parts of the canvas equally and had no visual center of attention. Although the press often derided Pollock as a purely impulsive and untrained artist, in reality he used careful calculation to achieve his allover compositions and to avoid emphasizing one area over another.

Although his dripping technique remained unchanged, Pollock reverted to figuration in 1951. In *Portrait and a Dream* (1953, Dallas Museum of Art, Texas), for example, interlaced streams of black paint on the left side of the canvas are fully abstract, but on the right side these black lines form a woman's head, which Pollock then filled in with patches of red, yellow, pink, and gray. He became less productive in the last years of his life, and died in an automobile accident in 1956.

Pollock's work proved remarkably influential on later artists: Colour-field painters Helen Frankenthaler and Morris Louis adapted his paint-pouring technique. Frank Stella and Robert Morris made allover composition a hallmark of the minimal art movement. Sculptors Richard Serra and Eva Hesse and performance artist Allan Kaprow retained Pollock's emphasis on the process of creation and pushed this emphasis even further.

Famous Work: *Number One 1948.*

❋❋

Lucian Freud

Lucian Freud, (1922-2011), English painter, known for his technical precision and distinguished by a talent for representing the human figure. Freud has played a vital role in the continuation of the tradition of portraiture in British painting.

The grandson of Austrian physician Sigmund Freud, he was born in Berlin but emigrated to England with his family as a child. Between 1939 and 1943 he trained at the Central School of Art in London, the East Anglian School of Painting and Drawing in Dedham, in eastern England, and Goldsmith's College in London. During the 1950s Freud became well-known internationally and was later given major retrospective exhibitions around the world.

Although in his youth Freud experimented with styles such as Surrealism and neo-romanticism, he found his own personal style through highly detailed realist (objective and unidealized) paintings such as the somber *Interior in Paddington* (1951, Walker Art Gallery, Liverpool, England). Many of his other works are also set in Paddington, the area of London in which he settled. Freud's later work, characterized by more expressive brushwork and greater tonal contrasts, includes a series of portraits of his mother.

Famous Work: *Girl with Roses.*

❊❊

Roy Lichtenstein

Roy Lichtenstein, (1923-1997), American painter, sculptor, and graphic artist, best-known for his large-scale paintings and prints based on comic strips. Along with fellow American artist Andy Warhol, Lichtenstein was one of the central figures of the American pop art movement in the 1960s, which celebrated popular, commercial images.

In the 1950s Lichtenstein painted works in a series of different styles. His subject matter also ranged from reproductions of 19th century paintings to commercial illustrations, and eventually comic strips. His trademark comic-book style dates from 1961, when he began to reproduce not only the subject matter but also the appearance of comic strips printed in newspapers. To accentuate the mass-produced quality of his cartoon heroines and fighter pilots, he imitated the newspaper printing style, using patterns of coloured dots to achieve different tones (fewer dots read as a lighter shade), a limited number of colours, and heavy black outlines.

Throughout his career he consistently applied these comic-strip conventions to a wide variety of subjects, including takeoffs on the paintings of other artists, large expressionistic brushstrokes, and architectural details. He created a series based on well-known works by modern European masters such as Pablo Picasso, Henri Matisse, and Claude Monet, and in 1996 based another series on Chinese landscape paintings.

In his ceramic and painted bronze sculptures, Lichtenstein used the same flattening, two-dimensional devices of his paintings to depict subjects ranging from explosions to goldfish bowls, cups with steam rising from them, and brushstrokes floating in the air.

Born in New York City, Lichtenstein began his artistic studies in 1939 with American artist Reginald Marsh at the Art Students League, New York City. He attended Ohio State University in Columbus, Ohio, where he earned his M.F.A. (Master of Fine Arts) degree in 1949. He stayed on to teach there for several years, and from 1957 taught at the State University of New York at Oswego. From 1960 to 1963 he taught at Douglass College in New Brunswick, New Jersey, where avant-garde artist Allan Kaprow introduced him to a form of performance art called *happenings,* and to the artists who created the form, including Claes Oldenburg and Jim Dine. Lichtenstein's first solo show of comic-strip paintings, at the Leo Castelli Gallery in New York City in 1962, was one of the first pop art exhibitions and created an art world sensation. In 1993 and 1994 the Solomon R. Guggenheim Museum, in New York City, held a retrospective exhibition of his work.

Famous Work: *Whaam!*

❊❊

Jasper Johns

Jasper Johns, American (1930-) one of the leading painters and designers of late 19th-century England, whose romantic paintings using medieval imagery were among the last manifestations of the Pre-Raphaelite style. More long-lasting is his influence as a pioneer of the revival of the ideal of the "artist-craftsman", so influential to 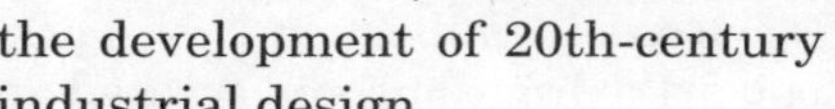 the development of 20th-century industrial design.

Burne-Jones was educated at Exeter College, Oxford, where he met his future collaborator, the artist-poet William Morris, then a fellow divinity student. His meeting with the artist Dante Gabriel Rossetti in 1856 marked a turning point in his career, and he left Oxford without graduating. Morris and he then settled in London, working under Rossetti's guidance.

Burne-Jones's vivid imagination delighted in the stories of medieval chivalry, as is seen in his "King Cophetua and the Beggar Maid" (1884) and "Merlin and Nimue" (1858–59). Stylistically, such works owe much to Rossetti's illustrations, but more often his own dreamworld drew inspiration from the melancholy, attenuated figures of the 15th-century Italian painters Filippino Lippi and Sandro Botticelli, suffusing them with a mood of romantic mysticism. His first big success came with an exhibition in 1877, which included oils such as "*Days of Creation*," "*The Beguiling of*

Merlin" (1872–77), and "*The Mirror of Venus*" (1867–77). From that date until his death, he was increasingly considered to be among the great painters of England. In 1894 he received a baronetcy.

After his death, Burne-Jones's influence was felt far less in painting than in the field of decorative design, particularly in that of ecclesiastical stained glass. He executed reliefs in metals, tiles, and gesso, decorations for pianos and organs, and cartoons for tapestries. Among the latter may be noted the "*Adoration of the Magi*" (Exeter College Chapel, Oxford). Besides several illustrations to other books printed by William Morris' prestigious Kelmscott Press, he made 87 designs for the Kelmscott *Chaucer* of 1896, considered to be among the world's finest printed books.

Famous Work: *Flag.*

❋❋

Andy Warhol

Andy Warhol, real name Andrew Warhola (1928-1987), American painter, motion-picture director and producer, and publisher, who was a leader of the pop art movement, which based artwork on images taken from mass, or popular, culture. Warhol is considered one of the most important American artists of the 20th century. His work and ideas both reflect and helped shape American mass media and popular culture.

Warhol was born in Pittsburgh, Pennsylvania, and educated at Carnegie Institute of Technology. During the 1950s Warhol practiced *commercial art* (art created primarily for promoting businesses) in New York City. He attracted attention in the 1960s with exhibitions of pop art subjects from daily life, such as *Campbell's Soup Can* (1965, Leo Castelli Gallery, New York City) and *Green Coca-Cola Bottles* (1962, Whitney Museum, New York City), and of popular entertainers such as Marilyn Monroe. These images were silk-screened, a mechanical process that allowed them to be endlessly repeated. Warhol took a similar impersonal approach in his experimental motion pictures. *Empire* (1964) provides an eight-hour view of the Empire State Building seen continuously from the same camera angle. *The Chelsea Girls* (1966), a seven-hour, virtually unedited film, features many of the actors from Warhol's

New York City studio known as the Factory. Improvised dialogue, lack of plot, and extreme eroticism were trademarks of *The Chelsea Girls* as well as of later, more complex films, such as *Lonesome Cowboys* (1969) and *Trash* (1970). In addition to working with art and motion pictures, Warhol helped promote the rock group Velvet Underground and produced the album *Velvet Underground with Nico* (1967).

Warhol's publications include *The Philosophy of Andy Warhol: From A to B and Back Again* (1975) and *America* (1985), a collection of his scathing photographs of contemporary life in the United States. From 1969 until his death, he published *Interview,* a monthly magazine with illustrated articles about current celebrities. In 1994 the Andy Warhol Museum, the largest single-artist museum in the United States, opened in Pittsburgh, Pennsylvania.

Famous Work: *Marilyn Monroe.*

❊❊

David Hockney

David Hockney, English (1937-) English painter, draftsman, printmaker, photographer, and stage designer whose works are characterized by economy of technique, a preoccupation with light, and a frank, mundane realism derived from Pop art and photography.

He studied at the Bradford College of Art (1953–57) and the Royal College of Art, London (1959–62), where he received a gold medal in the graduate competition. He visited the United States in 1961 and returned in 1964–67 to teach at the universities of Iowa, Colorado, and California, and thereafter commuted between England and the United States until settling permanently in Los Angeles in 1978. That city's intense, glaring light and sleek "California modern" aesthetic had a pronounced influence on his work.

Much of Hockney's subject matter is autobiographical, including portraits and self-portraits and quiet, incidental scenes of his friends and his quarters (*e.g., "Portrait of an Artist,"* 1971). The casual elegance and tranquil luminosity of these pieces also predominate in his still lifes. Hockney's exploration of photography in the 1980s resulted in *Pearblossom Hwy, 11–18th April 1986* and other ambitious photocollages. He published several series of graphic works in book form, including illustrations for *Six Fairy Tales of the Brothers Grimm* (1970) and *The Blue Guitar* (1977). Hockney also achieved international prominence as a stage-set designer for the opera and ballet. His books include *Hockney by Hockney* (1976), *Travels With Pen, Pencil, and Ink* (1978), *Paper Pools* (1980), *David Hockney Photographs* (1982), *China Diary* (1983), and *Hockney Paints the Stage* (1983).

Famous Work: *A Bigger Splash.*

❊❊

Damien Hirst

On Nov. 28, 1995, Damien Hirst was awarded the Turner Prize, Great Britain's most prestigious award for contemporary art. Whether Hirst's work indicated a new direction in British art was an open question, however, for while other avant-garde artists continued to work with traditional materials, Hirst's chosen means of expression for his best-known works was animals–dead or alive. In an exhibit at the Tate Gallery following his short-listing for the 1995 Turner (he was also short-listed in 1992), Hirst presented some of his classic pieces, including "*Mother and Child Divided*," a work consisting of four glass-and-steel tanks containing the severed halves of a cow and calf preserved in formalin, an aqueous formaldehyde solution. Some critics loved his work, while others accused him of striving only for shock value. Regardless of critical opinion, the Turner Prize established Hirst as one of Britain's most important new talents.

Hirst was born in Bristol in 1965 and grew up in Leeds. In the early 1980s he moved to London, where he worked in the building trades before studying art at Goldsmiths College. His early work included a series of dot paintings, as well as mixed-media sculpture. His career received a boost in 1988 when British advertising mogul Charles Saatchi attended an influential student show curated by Hirst. Saatchi subsequently became the leading collector of Hirst's work, purchasing a number of pieces, including "*A Thousand Years*," which consisted of a large tank containing a box of maggots, an electronic bug zapper, and a rotting cow's head on which the surviving flies laid more eggs.

In 1994 Hirst organized a show for young artists at the Serpentine Gallery in London, "*Some Went Mad, Some Ran Away...*" His contributions included "*The Physical Impossibility of Death in the Mind of Someone Living*," which consisted of a glass tank containing a 4.3-m (14-ft) tiger shark pickled in formaldehyde,

and "*Away from the Flock*," a lamb suspended in a similar tank. The show was a resounding success and garnered enormous publicity for Hirst, particularly when another artist poured ink into "*Away from the Flock*" and renamed it "*Black Sheep*."

Hirst attempted to stage a major exhibition in New York City in September 1995, but his plan for the centerpiece of the show – a display of dead cows that had not been preserved was forbidden by the New York Health Department. He returned to New York in 1996 with a new exhibit at the Gagosian Gallery. Entitled "*No Sense of Absolute Corruption*," this show presented some of Hirst's classic dead animals, as well as his newer work, including a series of large paintings done by pouring paint on a round canvas and then mechanically spinning it at a high rate of speed. Hirst also directed several short videos, notably a music video for the British rock group Blur.

Famous Work: *The Physical Impossibility of Death in the Mind of Someone Living (shark).*

❋❋